SPIRITS UNVEILED

A THEOLOGICAL UNVEILING OF THE SPIRITUAL REALM

BOOK TWO

By Tekoa Manning

www.manningthegatepublishing.com

Also, By Tekoa Manning

Walter: The Homeless Man: a novel

Polishing Jade: a novel

Thirsting for Water: a devotional

Jumping for Joy in the Midst of Sorrow: a devotional

The Spirit of Leviathan, Jezebel, and Athaliah: a teaching book.

Unmasking the Unseen Series:

Satan Unmasked: Book One

Spirits Unveiled: Book Two

Wolves Unseen: Book Three

King Revealed: Book Four

ISBN-13: 978-1-7374020-8-4 (Manning the Gate Publishing LLC)

Spirits Unveiled: Book Two Copyright © 2023 by Tekoa Manning

Unmasking the Unseen Series

All rights reserved.

The information in this book is based on the author's knowledge, research, education, experience, and opinions. The theology, exegesis, and hermeneutics described in this book are the author's opinions and theories. Your opinions may differ.

This work depicts actual events in the life of the author as truthfully as recollection permits and/or can be verified by research. Occasionally, dialogue consistent with the character or nature of the person speaking has been supplemented. All persons within are actual individuals; there are no composite characters. The names of some individuals have been changed to respect their privacy.

All trademarks appearing in this book are the property of their respective owners. This book may not be re-sold or given away to other people. If you'd like to share this book with another person, please purchase an additional copy for each person you share it with.

Copyright © 2023 Manning the Gate Publishing. All rights are reserved, including the right to reproduce this book or portions thereof. No part of this book may be reproduced in any form without the author's express written permission.

Editor – Jo Fouts Zausch

Narrator – Lynn Brunk

Cover by Lynette Marie Smith
Graphic Design & Marketing

Picture on Cover by francescoch

CONTENTS

Introduction ....

Chapter 1 ....

   The Witch of Endor Part 1 1

   The Witch of Endor Part 2 13

Chapter 2 ....

   Angelic Hosts Part 1 27

   Angelic Hosts Part 2 49

Chapter 3 ....

   Dry Places 67

Chapter 4 ....

   A Herd of Pigs 75

Chapter 5 ....

   Possession and Deliverance 87

Chapter 6 ....

   Heavenly Agents 99

Chapter 7 ....

   Semikhah, Laying on of Hands 109

Chapter 8 ....

   Binding the Spirits 123

Chapter 9 ....

   Unforgiveness and Demons 135

Chapter 10 ....
Sickness and Disease 143
Chapter 11...
Mental Illness... 163
Chapter 12 ....
The Accursed Thing 179
Chapter 13 ....
The Sins of the Fathers 191
Closing.. 207
Sources 213

Introduction

In 2015, my husband and I moved in with my father. My mother passed away a few years before, and we spent a year with him. On arriving, my father gave us the primary bedroom he and my mother had shared for years before her death. It was lovely, and the large windows showcased the fall leaves in all their burnt orange and vibrant yellows. When my husband and I arrived, we quickly cleaned and organized our things while respecting my dad's privacy and space. Shortly after we settled in, I awoke in the night with a strange spirit hovering over the bed. The figure was cloaked in a robe that was hooded. It seemed to be peering into my face. I had previously been involved in deliverance ministry, but this sight left me uneasy. I have seen a lot of things in my years, but never anything such as this.

I wondered who the spirit could represent or where it came from. My uncle, who stayed with my parents for a long time, left after a year or so and told others he could no longer stay there due to a ghost being in the house. My parents chuckled. My mother suffered horribly from Parkinson's before she passed away, but apparently, the spirit was already there when she was alive. How did it come about? My parents were devout Christians who had spent their lives doing ministry. Yes, this spirit was quite perplexing for me to grasp.

Demons are spirits we cast out and tell to "go" in the power and authority of Messiah Yeshua, but this, this cloaked hovering spirit, I found no words. I did not know what to make of it. And for fear that my husband would think I had lost my marbles, I did not bring it up for a few days, but this spirit in the night was bothering me. I prayed in the name of Messiah Yeshua for it to go, but it seemed not to budge. I had never had this experience when praying for tormented or oppressed people. A few more nights went by without me mentioning it to my husband, until one night, I sat down in a chair across from my husband and said, "I need to talk to you." He said, "okay, go right ahead." I started to fumble, getting my words together.

"Jeff, I hope you won't think I'm crazy or have imagination issues, but I have to talk to you about something that's happening in my dad's house." I looked him in the eye and waited for him to respond.

He said, "Is this concerning the figure cloaked in a robe over the bed at night?" I belted, "You saw it too?" He said, "yes, but I didn't want to scare you and was trying to figure out how to address it."

We finally decided to anoint the room with oil, pray over the house, and command whatever spirit was there to go to its resting place. However, again, the spirit did not leave. My husband and I were puzzled. We had never experienced this. Actually, we were the people that others called to pray over their homes when they sensed uneasiness.

One morning after a restless night, while my husband and I were praying, I asked the Father, "Why won't this robed spirit leave?" I heard in my spirit, "You have not been given authority here-- this is not your house." As soon as I heard this in my spirit, my dad walked into the room wearing his military greens, beret, and medals. He had been conducting a military funeral, and he was wearing authority. He was the homeowner. We asked my dad to have a seat on the bed and then began to inquire if he had seen a spirit. He said he had felt something strange but had never seen anything. We asked him if he would pray and ask the spirit to leave. He did, and it left. Where it went, I have no idea. Nor do I understand why it was hanging out in my mother and father's bedroom, but no one can convince my husband or me that we imagined it.

My husband and I believed our encounter with the robed being was a type of higher spiritual training. Jewish people often place a *mezuzah* on the outer doorframe at the front entrances of their homes while saying prayers of protection. A mezuzah is a piece of parchment rolled up and placed in a decorative case. The parchment has Deuteronomy 6:4–9 and a portion of Deuteronomy 11 written on it. While in Christianity, a pastor or priest typically walks from room to room, sprinkling each room with holy water and anointing the door frames with olive oil while reciting passages from the Gospel. When a home has strange occurrences and people believe that their house may have evil spirits in it, they will often call a pastor or priest to come to the house and rebuke the evil spirits and invite the Holy Spirit into the house while also counseling and praying for the members of the household. My husband and I realized the other homes we had prayed over were homes we had been invited to bless and pray for peace where there was no peace. We had not entered on our own accord without permission. Could this have been the reason why the spirit would not leave? Is there a hierarchy and an order to spirit beings? I believe it was no coincidence that my father entered the room in his military uniform while I was inquiring, and also, no coincidence that the spirit no longer was present in our bedroom at night. I now wondered if one of my parents had invited this spirit through ignorance or if there had been an old burial ground on the land, or some other reason for this spirit appearing. The Spirit Realm is primarily veiled.

In Isaiah 34 there is a peculiar passage about a spirit named Lilith:

> And spirits shall hold meetings in it, and an evil spirit shall call to his fellow. There a female night demon {Lilith} is rested, and she has found rest for herself.
>
> –Isaiah 34:14, AB

Isaiah's imagery is unsettling. The prophets often used heightened speech to make their points sharper, and Isaiah does just that as he describes the landscape in Chapter 34. He says the raven and owl will dwell in Edom along with the thistles and thorn bushes. Those, like Esau from which Edom gets its name, who sell their spiritual birthright for a bowl of red soup, or its equivalent, will live with the night demon. Isaiah describes dark demonic spirits that hold meetings, and to one, he gives the name *Lilith*. Lilith is first mentioned in an ancient Babylonian text concerning demonology. Lilith traveled from Babylon to the nations. According to Biblical Archeology, the ancient name "Lilith" derives from a Sumerian word for female demons or wind spirits—the *lilītu* and the related *ardat lilī*. Lilith is said to dwell in desert lands and open country spaces. Isaiah 34 is the only mention of her in the Bible. Dan Ben Amos, scholar and teacher, explains more *From Eden to Ednah Lilith in the Garden:*

> From demoness to Adam's first wife, Lilith has taken on many shapes over the millennia. She is first mentioned in ancient Babylonian texts as a class of winged female demons that attack pregnant women and infants. From Babylonia, the legend of "the Lilith" spread to ancient Anatolia, Syria, Israel, Egypt, and Greece. In this guise— as a wilderness demoness—she appears in Isaiah 34:14 among a list of nocturnal creatures who will haunt the destroyed kingdom of Edom. This is her only mention in

the Bible, but her legend continued to grow in ancient Judaism. During the Middle Ages, Jewish sources began to claim her as Adam's first—and terrifying—wife. [1]

As in the stories concerning Lilith, what has been taught about the spirit world is often not reality but mythology and tales passed down from one generation to another. Spirits and the spiritual world have captivated people since the beginning, and the stories concerning them have grown over time.

The Book of Job, said to be the oldest in the Bible, brings the reader into a front-row Cinemax viewing of a spiritual world. Job's friend mentions his interaction with this spiritual world that causes his hair to stand up:

> Now a word was brought to me stealthily; my ear received the whisper of it. Amid thoughts from visions of the night, when deep sleep falls on men, dread came upon me and trembling, which made all my bones shake. A spirit glided past my face; the hair of my flesh stood up. It stood still, but I could not discern its appearance. A form was before my eyes; there was silence, then I heard a voice: 'Can mortal man be in the right before God? Can a man be pure before his Maker?
>
> –Job 4:12-17, ESV

---

[1] Lilith in the Bible and Mythology - Biblical Archaeology Society

In this passage, Job's friend, Eliphaz the Temanite, says a spirit glided past his face. At times we get a glimpse into the spirit world, but what do we know about the ancient writings concerning the Spiritual Realm? How much of the text in our Bibles concerning spirits has been exaggerated or embellished over time? The 1st-century Jewish historian Josephus mentions demons and exorcisms in his writings and describes them as both an ancient and modern practice. The Messiah knew about spirits and ghosts, for he spoke of them:

> Why are you troubled, and why do doubts arise in your hearts? See my hands and my feet, that it is I myself. Touch me, and see. For a spirit does not have flesh and bones as you see that I have.
>
> –Luke 24:38-39, ESV

According to Luke 24, the belief in spirits in Yeshua's day was alive and well. Even today, with such depths of darkness portrayed in horror films and many occult-type books hosting incantations and spells, we find every religion has its own spin or belief concerning a hierarchy of demons and the shadows that wake us in the night. The Jewish virtual library has an interesting article *Dibbuk* which details the folklore and evolution of the *dibbukim* on (evil spirits):

> In Jewish folklore and popular belief, an evil spirit which enters into a living person, cleaves to his soul, causes mental illness, talks through his mouth, and represents a

separate and alien personality is called a *dibbuk*. The term appears neither in Talmudic literature nor in the Kabbalah, where this phenomenon is always called "evil spirit." (In Talmudic literature, it is sometimes called *ru'aḥ tezazit,* and in the New Testament *unclean spirit.*) The term was introduced into literature only in the 17th century from the spoken language of German and Polish Jews. [2]

By the second temple period and the writings of the New Testament, especially in the Gospels, we see an overwhelming number of references to demons. In Hellenism and Jewish folklore, many believed the demons were dead spirits seeking rest or that evil spirits entered the bodies of sick people because of sins. As time went on, adding to these beliefs was widespread fear of opening the door to a spirit realm because of committing sins or so-called generational curses. Yeshua corrects his disciples concerning such ignorance:

> And his disciples asked him, "Rabbi, who sinned, this man or his parents, that he was born blind?" Jesus answered, "It was not that this man sinned, or his parents, but that the works of God might be displayed in him.'"
>
> –John 9:2-3, ESV

---

[2] Dibbuk (Dybbuk) (jewishvirtuallibrary.org)

Also, in the Bible, there are references to spirits that linger in the darkness, and a large amount of context concerning angelic beings appears. The passages concerning angels are both mystical and enlightening. Multiple books of the Bible highlight these divine beings. This book, Book II, *Spirits Unveiled*, presents a more comprehensive investigation of the passages in the Bible where spirits are mentioned. It also covers who sends the spirits, both angelic and demonic, and the messengers who are often mistaken as angels but are, in all actuality, men. This revelation may require new wineskins and an open mind from the reader to remove doctrines of men that have crept in over time.

Chapter 1

THE WITCH OF ENDOR
PART 1

In I Samuel 28, a witch, a king, and a prophet are highlighted. This story has many interesting points to ponder involving the spirit realm. The story ends with a defeated king who gets a death sentence and then curiously, like the prodigal son, the king eats a fattened calf and unleavened bread with a witch. To set the scene, the mighty prophet Samuel has died. King Saul is bloodthirsty. He is chasing David, but David has gone to the enemy's territory, the Philistines. The Philistines gathered their armed forces to fight against King Saul, and Adonai orchestrated it. Saul has been disobedient. Saul, who was anointed by Samuel and given the crown, can no longer hear from the Holy One. "When Saul inquired of *Adonai, Adonai* did not answer, neither by dreams nor by Urim or prophets" (I Samuel 28:6, TLV).

The king is frightened. He needs to know the future. Will he lose the title? Will the Philistines destroy the armies of Israel? Like a silly girl reading her horoscope, Saul wants answers now but can no longer hear the Father's Voice. At first crowning, King Saul removed witchcraft from the land, according to the Torah. "You must not permit a sorceress to live" (Exodus 22:17, TLV). Now that the Holy One has shut out all contact, Saul is desperate. The first thing he does is seek out a necromancer to speak with the dead. Unlike Lazarus, who came out of the grave and removed his grave clothes at Yeshua's authority, the necromancers have no such power. Those who delve into necromancy were commanded to be put to death. The prophet Isaiah clearly explains:

> Here I am with the children that *Adonai* has given me as signs and wonders in Israel, from *Adonai-Tzva'ot* who dwells on Mount Zion. When they say to you: "Consult the mediums and necromancers who chirp and mutter," shouldn't a people seek their God? Should a people consult the dead on behalf of the living? To *Torah* and to the testimony!
>
> –Isaiah 8:18-20, TLV

In fact, people have always wondered about death and the afterlife. More recently, people having "after death" experiences have become widespread and often shared via YouTube. Hollywood made a movie about one young boy after his so-called heavenly experience. In II Corinthians 12, the Apostle Paul had an after-death experience after being stoned to death in the streets of Lystra. He was dragged through the city gate, cast outside the walls, and left to die. Paul explains later that he saw the 3rd heavens, but Paul was forbidden to speak of such matters, and he warns others should not either:

> I know a man in Messiah (whether in the body I don't know, or whether out of the body I don't know—God knows)—fourteen years ago, he [Paul] was caught up to the third heaven. I know such a man (whether in the body or outside of the body I don't know—God knows)— he was caught up into Paradise and heard words too sacred to tell, which a human is not permitted to utter.
>
> –II Corinthians 12:2-3, TLV

Paul was able to experience a realm most humans never see. The witch of Endor is trying to tap into the underworld, Sheol, the grave. This occultic practice has its roots in shamanism. Shamans are said to achieve various powers through trance or ecstatic religious experiences. Isaiah 8 reveals the sound the necromancers made by muttering and chirping to gain access to the spirits of the dead. "When they say to you: 'Consult the mediums and necromancers who chirp and mutter,' shouldn't a people seek their God? Should a people consult the dead on behalf of the living? To *Torah* and to the testimony!" (Isaiah 8:19, TLV).

The witch of Endor's practice was to seek the dead, those who had departed and attempt to receive information from them. The prophet warns that God's people were to seek Him. King Saul disguises himself, changes his clothing, takes two men, and approaches the Witch of Endor at night for information. One may dabble in these things, ignorantly knowing no better, but the king knew better. Saul had to write the Torah and keep his own copy. King Saul had already warned that he would cut off the witches in the land. Now, he is so desperate, like Esau trading his birthright for some lentil soup, Saul has sunk into the mire. Even the Witch of Endor gives him a means of escape, but he does not take it. Saul, instead, makes a vow by the Holy One that he will spare her life if she obeys him instead of the Holy One. Concerning the commandments, every matter is established by the testimony of two or three witnesses, and Saul has brought two men, and there is, of course, the Witch, making three (John 8:17, Deuteronomy 17:6). Saul begs and pleads for her to conjure up a ghost—Samuel. Again, notice, that the Witch gives the king a way of escape:

> "Look, you know what Saul has done," she said, "how he has cut off the mediums and spiritists from the land. So why then are you setting a trap for my life to get me killed?" Saul vowed to her by *Adonai* saying, "As *Adonai* lives, no punishment will come on you for this thing." "Whom will I bring up for you?" the woman asked. "Bring me up Samuel," he said.
>
> –I Samuel 28:9-11, TLV

This particular story has been interpreted in several ways. Some theologians state that the witch did not bring up Samuel and was acting as a ventriloquist. *The Jewish Encyclopedia* says that the Septuagint translated the word *necromancy* as one like a ventriloquist. *History Things* website shares the origins of ventriloquism in their article, *Take A Look Into the Dark History of Ventriloquism:*

> In Latin, the word (ventriloquist) stems from something that "speaks from the stomach," which the Greeks went on to describe as *gastromancy*, an act directly related to necromancy. In this light, the ventriloquist was viewed as a figure who could speak to the dead and, subsequently, have them speak to the living. They were a go between for the dead and living and for many people, this was simply too dark an idea to conceive. [3]

It is thought that necromancy's origins go back to the Stone Age practice of ancestor worship. The Holy One forbids it regardless of when it evolved or what type of black magic it is categorized under.

Multiple theological arguments have arisen concerning whether the prophet Samuel's spirit indeed stood before King Saul or if it was a demonic entity. However, the passages from I Samuel 28 are quite revealing. The Holy One gave a promise to

---

[3] Take A Look Into the Dark History of Ventriloquism (historythings.com)

Samuel when He anointed him. The Holy One told Samuel that none of his prophetic words would fall to the ground. "So Samuel grew, and the Lord was with him and let none of his words fall to the ground" (I Samuel 3:19, NKJ). Did Samuel prophesy to Saul one last time from the grave? The Bible tells us he did:

> "Whom will I bring up for you?" the woman asked. "Bring me up Samuel," he said. But when the woman saw Samuel, she cried out with a loud shriek. Then the woman spoke to Saul saying, "Why have you deceived me? You are Saul!" "Don't be afraid!" the king said to her. "What do you see?" The woman said to Saul, "I see a godlike being coming up from the earth." "What does he look like?" he asked her. "An old man is coming up, and he is wrapped with a robe," she said. Then Saul knew that it was Samuel, so he bowed down and prostrated himself with his face to the ground.
>
> —I Samuel 28:11-14, TLV

The woman, known to the surrounding area as a necromancer, is not used to seeing what she sees—she cries out with a loud shriek. Saul cannot see Samuel, but the woman's description causes him to believe with a knowing it is Samuel by his mantle. Samuel asked Saul why he had disturbed him from his rest in Sheol. The author of the Book of I Samuel is thought to be Samuel, and after his death, according to scholars, the prophet Nathan and the prophet Gad more than likely authored the remaining portions of I and II Samuel. Would not the prophets have informed the reader that it was not Samuel but a dark spirit imitating Samuel? Instead, the passage states that Saul knew it was Samuel.

Continuing in I Samuel 28, the prophet Samuel gives Saul a harsh proclamation concerning his battle against the Philistines. Samuel then prophesies Saul's death and the death of his sons. Saul is in distress. He tells Samuel that the Holy One has cast him away. The prophet informs Saul that he will be where he is tomorrow, in Sheol:

> Samuel said, "So why ask me, since *Adonai* has turned away from you and become your adversary? Now *Adonai* has done for Himself just as He foretold through me—*Adonai* has torn the kingship out of your hand and has given it to another fellow, to David. Since you did not obey the voice of *Adonai* and did not execute His fierce wrath on Amalek, so *Adonai* has done this to you today. Moreover, *Adonai* will also give the Israelites who are with you into the hand of the Philistines. Tomorrow you and your sons will be with me! Yes, *Adonai* will give the army of Israel into the hand of the Philistines.'"
>
> –I Samuel 28:15-19, TLV

The message from I Samuel 28:17 concerning the Lord taking the Kingship from Saul is accurate when compared to Samuel's earlier words in I Samuel 15:28: "So Samuel said to him [Saul], 'The LORD has torn the kingdom of Israel from you today, and has given it to a neighbor of yours, *who is* better than you.'"(NKJ) Not only does Samuel predict that Saul will be in the place of departed spirits, but his sons will also. "So Saul, his three sons, his armorbearer, and all his men died together that same day" (I Samuel 31:6, NKJ). Witches and false prophets only prophesy smooth words, itching ear words, words they know people, especially those in positions of power, want to hear. Sure, even sorcerers can predict some things accurately. The Egyptians could perform magic, but Samuel speaks the truth to Saul. The false prophets and sorcerers mutter and peep. In I Kings 22, the ratio of false prophets to true prophets is four hundred to one:

> Then the king of Israel gathered the prophets together, about four hundred men, and said to them, "Shall I go against Ramoth Gilead to fight, or shall I refrain?"
>
> So they said, "Go up, for the Lord will deliver *it* into the hand of the king."
>
> And Jehoshaphat said, "*Is there* not still a prophet of the Lord here, that we may inquire of Him?"
>
> So the king of Israel said to Jehoshaphat, "*There is* still one man, Micaiah the son of Imlah, by whom we may

inquire of the Lord; but I hate him, because he does not prophesy good concerning me, but evil."

–I Kings 22:6-8, NKJ

In I Kings 22, all the false prophets told the kings that they would be prosperous and defeat their enemies, all but one who predicted the death of the king of Israel. He spoke the truth, but the king could not bear hearing it. Samuel's spirit is speaking the truth to Saul. Many witches and wiccans involved in black magic cast spells and incantations using curses. Those who seek the darkness and the hidden realm of death cannot bring forth life, blessings, or light. They present crystals that give energy, yoga, tarot cards, chakras, and channeling. The process of channeling is often used by psychics, necromancers, and mediums for the purpose of obtaining knowledge from non-physical entities, spirit guides, or from one's own higher self-consciousness. Unknowingly, the New Age belief is empty and those teaching and practicing it reside in a spiritual place of death. The prophet Samuel tells Saul that Saul and his sons will die and be with him in the abode of the dead the next day. Not one of Samuel's words fell to the ground, according to I Samuel 3:19. And what does Saul do after he receives the fearful word from Samuel? After Samuel departs, Saul is weakened and full of fear. The witch offers him a meal—a fat calf:

> But he refused and said, "I won't eat." But when his courtiers and the woman urged him, he listened to them.

> So he got up from the ground and sat on the bed. The woman had a fatted calf in the house, so she hurried and butchered it, and took flour, kneaded it, and baked unleavened bread from it. She brought it before Saul and his courtiers, and they ate. Then they arose and went away that night.
>
> –I Samuel 28:23-25, TLV

This story of Saul is true but also an allegory and example of what happens when a person turns away from the Lord and sins against Him. A similar meal is shared between Abraham and three divine messengers who appear. Abraham was waiting patiently on the Holy One. He was not seeking answers from witches as to why his wife was still barren. When the angels show up, Abraham does what the witch of Endor did. He prepares a feast. But oh, what contrast:

> So Abraham hurried into the tent and said to Sarah, "Quick! Prepare three seahs of fine flour, knead it, and bake some bread." Meanwhile, Abraham ran to the herd, selected a tender and choice calf, and gave it to a servant, who hurried to prepare it. Then Abraham brought curds and milk and the calf that had been prepared, and he set them before the men and stood by them under the tree as they ate.
>
> –Genesis 18:6-8, BSB

The angels inform Abraham that his wife Sarah will give birth to a son around that time next year. The men gave a prophecy concerning Isaac and the seed of Abraham. There is another story where a fattened calf is highlighted. It's the story of the prodigal son. The son leaves the safety of his father's house, takes his inheritance, and travels far away. He ends up penniless and wishing to eat what the pigs ate. Finally, he comes to his senses, leaves that place, and returns home to his father. He confesses that he has sinned and is no longer worthy of being called his son, but the father is merciful and full of love. The father has a fattened calf prepared:

> But the father said to his servants, "Bring out the best robe and put *it* on him, and put a ring on his hand and sandals on *his* feet. And bring the fatted calf here and kill *it,* and let us eat and be merry; for this my son was dead and is alive again; he was lost and is found." And they began to be merry.
>
> Now his older son was in the field. And as he came and drew near to the house, he heard music and dancing. So he called one of the servants and asked what these things meant. And he said to him, "Your brother has come, and because he has received him safe and sound, your father has killed the fatted calf."
>
> –Luke 15:22-27, NKJ

Chapter 1

THE WITCH OF ENDOR
PART 2

Throughout scripture, the fatted calf is a symbol of God's favor and a celebration, a festival. Saul does the complete opposite of Abraham and the prodigal. Saul started humble and small in his own eyes (I Sam. 15:17). The Book of Samuel says Saul received a new heart in one day (I Sam. 10:1,9). Saul is crowned king, and he is honored by the people. He is anointed by the holy prophet Samuel. He has removed the witchcraft from the land. By the end of Saul's life, his heart is full of murder. He is full of pride. The king can no longer hear from Adonai. Saul then trades his kingly garments, signet ring, and shoes of peace for a disguise. The king then seeks a witch. After he hears the fearful words of Samuel, Saul sits on the witch's bed, a place of intimacy, and dines on her delicacies. She has killed the choice calf and kneaded the dough. Proverbs 9 mentions two women, the harlot, and her delicacies, or the righteous woman and her wisdom:

> Wisdom has built her house. She has carved out her seven pillars. She has slaughtered her meat, she has mixed her wine; she has also set her table. She has sent out her servant girls. She calls from the city's heights: "Whoever is naïve, turn in here!" To those who lack understanding, she says: "Come, eat my bread and drink the wine I have mixed. Abandon your foolish ways and live! Walk in the way of understanding."
>
> –Proverbs 9:1-6, TLV

The wise woman has carved out seven pillars. This is the seven Spirits of Adonai according to the Book of Isaiah, Isaiah 11:2:

1. The Spirit of wisdom

2. The Spirit of the Lord

3. The Spirit of understanding

4. The Spirit of counsel

5. The Spirit of power

6. The Spirit of knowledge

7. The Spirit of the fear of the Lord

The harlot mentioned in Proverbs 7 below has enticed King Saul. A person is warned to keep the commandments and to make them as the apple of the eye, to not be enticed by the smooth lips of the harlot. Her ways lead only to death:

With her persistent pleading she entices him, with smooth talk she seduces him. Suddenly he follows her like an ox going to the slaughter, like a stag bounding toward a trap, till an arrow pierces its liver. Like a bird darting into a snare, he never considered his own soul! Now then, sons, listen to me, pay attention to the words of my mouth.

Do not let your heart turn to her ways or stray onto her paths. For many are the victims she has brought down, and numerous are all her slain. Her house is a highway to *Sheol*, leading down to the chambers of death.

–Proverbs 7:21-27, TLV

Interestingly, the pierced liver, mentioned in Proverbs 7, and kidneys symbolize human emotions and the conscience, not the heart. In Hebrew thought, the heart has to do with the mind. The prophet explains our condition: "You are near in their mouth but far from their kidneys" (Jeremiah 12:2, ISR). Our Bible translators have replaced the word *kidney* with *rein* or *heart* and often as *inward parts*, but kidneys were the original wording. It was the sweet fat of the sacrifices. Our kidneys purify us. They separate the good from the bad:

> The position of the kidneys in the body makes them particularly inaccessible, and in cutting up an animal, they are the last organs to be reached. Consequently, they were a natural symbol for the most hidden part of a

man (Psalm 139:13), and in Job 16:13 to "cleave the reins asunder" is to affect the total destruction of the individual (compare Job 19:27 Lamentations 3:13). This hidden location, coupled with the sacred sacrificial use, caused the kidneys to be thought of as the seat of the innermost moral (and emotional) impulses. [4]

I Samuel 15 describes Saul's kidneys as being full of toxins. The Holy One tells Samuel that He regrets making Saul king and that Saul has been disobedient. Samuel informs Saul that he used to be humble but now has grown prideful. Samuel confronts Saul on how he kept the spoils of the enemy and did not carry out his assignment. Saul admits he has sinned and violated the commands of the Holy One. Saul responds: "I feared the people and listened to their voice" (I Samuel 15:24, NASB). Saul sought accolades from men more than honor from God. Saul is likened to the ox headed for slaughter in Proverbs 7. King Saul never considered his own soul--no, not even the souls of his sons.

As the battle against the Philistines continued, Saul knew he was defeated. He asked a young man to pierce him with his sword, but he would not. As the battle raged on, Saul became severely wounded by the Philistines. Saul then falls upon his sword to kill himself, but this is not the end of the matter; it's far more gruesome:

---

[4] Topical Bible: Kidneys (biblehub.com)

The next day, when the Philistines came to strip the dead, they found Saul and his three sons fallen on Mount Gilboa. They cut off Saul's head, stripped off his armor, and sent messengers throughout the land of the Philistines to proclaim the news in the temples of their idols and among their people. They put his armor in the temple of the Ashtoreth and hung his body on the wall of Beth-shan.

–I Samuel 31:8-10, BSB

Saul became so seduced by the harlot's smooth tongue whispering in his ear that he lost everything, including his head. At the news of the king's death, David mourns Saul and his sons, especially Jonathan, whom he loved dearly. David speaks wise words and blessings over his enemy.

When studying Saul's life, there is much to learn. It is the complete story of salvation, new life, a new heart, the anointing that breaks the yoke, favor, and positions of power. The wages of sin lead to death. Saul's kingship is severed, and his headship is cut off. Saul became disobedient. He became full of himself and more concerned about people pleasing than pleasing the Father. He became complacent and could no longer hear from God, the holy prophets, or in dreams, so he sought the darkness -- a witch. What a pitiful condition to find oneself in. This backslidden condition led to more and more darkness and, eventually, a horrible death. The Bible describes disobedience and rebellion unto the Lord as witchcraft:

> For rebellion *is as* the sin of witchcraft, And stubbornness *is as* iniquity and idolatry. Because you have rejected the word of the LORD, He also has rejected you from *being* king.
>
> –I Samuel 15:23-24, NKJ

Rebellion and witchcraft go together. Saul and the witch of Endor paints a picture for all of us. We can travel far away from the Holy One--so far; indeed, we end up in a pigsty like the prodigal son. Saul was not genuinely repentant; he was sorry he got caught. Many are ignorant and dine on meals prepared by witches. Believers are often ignorant of witchcraft and unaware that they are feeding their children the fattened calf prepared by the witch of Endor.

Today witchcraft is on the rise. The number of witches and Americans practicing Wicca religious rituals has skyrocketed. *News Week* blog site gives detailed statistics in an article titled *Number of Witches Rises Dramatically Across U.S as Millennials Reject Christianity.* Author Benjamin Fearnow stated that a Trinity College study found approximately 8,000 practicing Wiccans in the United States in the 1990s compared to over 1.5 million practicing witches in 2018. Benjamin quoted Julie Roys, who provides insight into the reasons for Wiccan growth:

"The rejection of Christianity has left a void that people, as inherently spiritual beings, will seek to fill," author Julie Roys said in comments emailed to *The Christian Post* last month. "Plus, Wicca has effectively repackaged witchcraft for millennial consumption," Roys continued. "No longer is witchcraft and paganism satanic and demonic; it's a 'pre-Christian tradition' that promotes 'free thought' and 'understanding of earth and nature.'"

Roys is correct. Witchcraft is now repackaged and called good. Many Christians practice holidays that are rooted in paganism ignorantly. As the younger generation has become more knowledgeable concerning the origins of Easter, Halloween, and Christmas traditions being rooted in paganism, they feel Christianity has lied to them, or they do not know what to believe. With so many voices today infiltrating the media, I advise researching like the Bereans (Acts 17:11) to see if what you are being taught is correct, and that includes this book.

The Book of Jeremiah warns Israel not to learn the way of the nations. The prophet Isaiah warns against mixing the holy with the profane and for calling evil good: "Woe (judgment is coming) to those who call evil good, and good evil; Who substitute darkness for light and light for darkness; Who substitute bitter for sweet and sweet for bitter!" (Isaiah 5:20, A.P.). Children's books today are full of witchcraft, incantations, and all kinds of New Age garb. A recent (2022) Halloween commercial for *Twix* candy bars/ *Mars* company showcased an Ouija Board--a tool witches use to communicate with spirits and the dead. The commercial showed children sitting around the board playing and watching the letters fly through the air—child's play. Mars makes M&M's, Snickers, Dove bars, and a whole host of candy.

We must become aware of who we give our money to and what we allow our children to be entertained by on their cell phones, computers, and television screens. When I was a child, *Bewitched* aired on television, starring Elizabeth Montgomery. She was a beautiful witch named Samantha who married a mortal named Darrin Stephens. My mother was not on board when this first aired, but the comedy soon spread and became a hit show. Magic and spells were used in ways that made them appear needed, harmless, and a tool for fixing things that were going wrong. The 1990s gave way to a sitcom named *Charmed* which depicted three sisters who were "good witches" and had abilities to defeat demons and evil beings. *Picket Fences, Buffy the Vampire Slayer*, and other television shows began to present both Wiccans and witches in a wonderful light. In these series, the characters who were Wiccans or witches held power against evil, not the righteous.

A popular movie, *The Craft*, had actual witches on set. According to *Time magazine, The Craft* inspired a generation of teenage witches. Author Peg Aloi's article *The Craft Inspired a*

Generation of Teenage Witches. Now a Sequel Is Poised to Do the Same is quite the eye-opener:

> The production employed an adviser, Pat Devin, a practicing witch, high priestess of Gardnerian Wicca (also known as modern pagan witchcraft), and Chief Information Officer for the religious organization *The Covenant of the Goddess*. Interviewed in 1997 about the experience, Devin described her efforts to improve the image of witches in the film: "My goal for the rituals and chants was that they be authentic, if generic, and that they contain nothing that could not be easily found in at least two books, or plausibly created by teenage girls.'"

When adults dress their cute four-year-old in a witches costume at Halloween and the child smiles up at the person handing them candy, again, child's play. "You must not turn to mediums or spiritists; do not seek them out, or you will be defiled by them. I am the LORD your God" (Leviticus 19:31, BSB). We, the believers in Yeshua Messiah are supposed to talk to our children about our Father's Commandments/Torah when we sit and rise (Deut. 11:19). Oh, how sad. The things we have allowed in our homes started years and years ago. Witchcraft today is enticing the younger generation and becoming a billion-dollar industry. The sorcery is dressed up and made entertaining, but I assure you it's anything but. Do not be deceived by "white witches" or New Age tactics packaged to suggest one can resurrect their spiritual side and gain cosmic energy, crystal power, and Reiki healing. There is only one true Spirit that can resurrect the dead and that is the Breath of the Almighty God, the Ruach HaKodesh (Holy Spirit).

The Conversation, a blog site featuring scholarly articles, has a jaw-dropping post written by Nicole Lenoir-Jourdan, Ph.D. candidate and author at Deakin University, *How Witchcraft Became a multi-billion Dollar Industry*.

1. In 2018, cosmetics giant *Sephora* launched their US$42 "Starter Witch Kit," containing sage, tarot cards, and rose quartz. After witches around the globe decried it as cultural appropriation, *Sephora* pulled the product from the market.

2. Savvy witches are thriving on the internet. *#witchtok* on *TikTok* has had over 5.3 billion views, and *#witchesofinstagram* has more than 5.5 million posts. You can buy over 400,000 products tagged "*witch*" on *Etsy*, from candles to spell bottles to pentagram necklaces.

3. *Urban Outfitters* sell smudge sticks, tarot cards, and crystals in their U.S. stores and witch hat incense holders in Australian outlets. *Booktopia* sells tarot cards. [5]

---

[5] How witchcraft became a multi-billion dollar industry (theconversation.com)

Protect your children. Seek life even if you are mocked and called an ignorant fanatic or a cult follower. Do not be led astray like King Saul and others. Even if someone tells you these things are harmless, they are not.

Frances Schaefer, evangelical theologian, philosopher, and Presbyterian pastor was spot on when he said:

> If there is no absolute moral standard, then one cannot say in a final sense that anything is right or wrong. By absolute, we mean that which always applies, that which provides a final or ultimate standard. There must be an absolute if there are to be morals, and there must be an absolute if there are to be real values. If there is no absolute beyond man's ideas, then there is no final appeal to judge between individuals and groups whose moral judgments conflict. We are merely left with conflicting opinions. [6]

There is no conflicting opinion concerning God's Word, for His Word is true:

> Whoever turns to mediums or spiritists to prostitute himself with them, I will also set My face against that person and cut him off from his people.
>
> –Leviticus 20:6, BSB

---

[6] Francis Schaeffer quote: If there is no absolute moral standard, then one cannot... (azquotes.com)

Those who believe in the God of Abraham, Isaac, and Jacob must stand up and become educated. Even the anointed can be led astray, enticed, becoming rebellious and disobedient. May King Saul's last supper prepared by a witch be an example for all of us.

Spirits Unveiled: Book Two

Chapter 2
ANGELIC HOSTS
PART 1

Angelic Beings are mysterious, but many have encountered them on their journey unawares. The Book of Hebrews reminds us of this. "Do not neglect to show hospitality to strangers, for by so doing some people have entertained angels without knowing it" (Hebrews 13:2, BSB).

Once when my grandparents were getting ready for bed, they heard a faint knock on the door. On opening, my grandfather was greeted by a stranger in the snow. It had been snowing steadily for hours, and the man seemed to need shelter. My grandparents lived on much acreage in a small town in Kentucky. They had twelve children, including two sons who fought in World War II. They were hospitable people, who welcomed the stranger in, stroked the fire, warmed up leftovers, and had a pleasant lengthy conversation with the man before settling him on the couch for the night. Once in their own bed, my grandfather mentioned to my grandmother the man's eyes and how warm and endearing he was. My grandmother agreed and brought up the conversation the three of them had had. "Albert," she said to my grandfather, "it's as if the man knew all our problems and the things we have been praying for." Yes, the strange fellow quoted the Bible and smiled warmly at them as though he understood what was happening in their lives. The following day the man appeared to be gone. My grandfather opened the door to see if he'd left, and there were no footprints - in fact, not a single set of prints were to be found in the snow of his 200-acre farm. In the corner of the living room sat the man's shoes. The shoes looked as if they had never been worn.

Angelic beings are mysterious. These messengers reveal God's plans and obey His will. Over time these heavenly hosts have taken on many forms and hierarchical rankings:

> Now it came to pass when Joshua was near Jericho that he lifted up his eyes and looked, and behold, there was a man standing in front of him with his sword drawn in his hand. Joshua approached him and said to him: "Are you for us or for our adversaries?" "Neither," he said. "Rather, I have now come as commander of Adonai's army."
>
> Then Joshua fell on his face to the ground and worshipped. Then he asked him, "What is my lord saying to his servant?" Then the commander of Adonai's army replied to Joshua, "Take your sandal off of your foot, for

> the place where you are standing is holy." And Joshua did so.
>
> —Joshua 5:13-15, TLV

A similar story is told in Exodus 3. Both Moses and Joshua must remove their footwear:

> When Adonai saw that he (Moses) turned to look, He called to him out of the midst of the bush and said, "Moses, Moses!" So he answered, "Hineni." Then He said, "Come no closer. Take your sandals off your feet, for the place where you are standing is holy ground." Moreover, He said, "I am the God of your father, the God of Abraham, Isaac and Jacob." So Moses hid his face, because he was afraid to look at God.
>
> —Exodus 3:4-5, TLV

In Exodus 3, Moses hides his face from Adonai. Later in the story, after Moses spends much time with Adonai on Mount Sinai receiving the Torah (Commandments), Moses has to cover his face because the Children of Israel are scared to look upon him:

> And when Moses came down from Mount Sinai with the two tablets of the Testimony in his hands, he was unaware that his face had become radiant from speaking with the LORD. Aaron and all the Israelites looked at Moses, and behold, his face was radiant. And they were afraid to

approach him.

–Exodus 34:35, BSB

Both stories hold many similarities and metaphors. Moses is told to remove his sandals. In Joshua 5, it is worded sandal, singular, and foot, not feet, which many scholars have argued over the semantics of. However, I want to expound on other points.

Both Exodus 3 and Joshua 5 contain similarities:

1. Circumcision of Moses' sons in the wilderness by Zipporah (bird/dove)

2. Israel kept the Passover/Pesach, but after the first year in the wilderness, the Passover was never celebrated again until Israel crossed over into the Promised Land.

3. Manna/ then first fruits of Canaan

4. Removal of sandals

In Joshua 5, he encounters a man and wonders whose side he is on concerning the battle. Once the angelic messenger informs him that he is the Commander of Adonai's Army, Joshua falls on his face. This happens right after all the men of war died out -- the men who had not listened to the Voice of Adonai:

> Then Adonai said to Joshua, "This day, I have rolled away the reproach of Egypt from you." Therefore the name of that place has been called Gilgal to this day. While Bnei-

Yisrael camped at Gilgal, they observed Passover on the evening of the fourteenth day of the month in the plains of Jericho. On the day after the Passover, on that very day, they ate of the produce of the land, matzot and roasted grain.

–Joshua 5:9-11, TLV

These stories in Exodus and Joshua concern our Messiah, Yeshua, whose shining face, salvation, and burnished bronze feet are captured throughout.

According to Abarim publications:

"The name Gilgal comes from the Hebrew verb גלל (galal), meaning to roll or roll away. After Joshua had circumcised Israel, God said that he had rolled away the reproach of Egypt. . . Note that the name Gilgal is spelled the same as the nouns galgal and gilgal that were derived of the verb galal. Noun גלגלת (gulgoleth) means skull or head."

Remember Golgotha translated as (Place of a Skull). This is where they crucified our King. Gilgal has several meanings "to roll," as Yahweh said he was rolling away their reproach of Egypt/sin. Another meaning of Gilgal is (gil) joy and celebration. I like to think of the stone being rolled away from the tomb and how Yeshua's death brought resurrection, life, and redemption:

They found the stone rolled away from the tomb, but

when they entered, they did not find the body of the Lord Jesus. While they were puzzling over this, suddenly two men in radiant apparel stood beside them. As the women bowed their faces to the ground in terror, the two men asked them, "Why do you look for the living among the dead? He is not here; He has risen!

–Luke 24:3-6, BSB

Moses had to remove his sandals because he was standing on holy "ground." Joshua had to remove his sandal on holy "land." He was like Boaz, who removed his sandal to take Ruth, a Moabite as his bride. Yeshua is our kinsman redeemer:

> Now in former times in Israel, concerning the redemption or exchange of property, to make any matter legally binding, a man would remove his sandal and give it to the other party, and this was a confirmation in Israel. So the kinsman-redeemer removed his sandal and said to Boaz, "Buy it for yourself."
>
> –Ruth 4:7-8, BSB

John, the immerser in Luke 3, said that he baptized with water, but One more powerful than him would come, One whose straps of his sandals John was not worthy to untie. John told the people Yeshua would baptize or immerse them in fire and the Ruach HaKodesh (Holy Spirit).

This is none other than Yeshua, the cloud by day, the fire by night, the burning bush, removing the shoes. By the end of the Book, John the Revelator describes Yeshua:

> In the midst of the menorot, I saw One like a Son of Man, clothed in a robe down to His feet, with a golden belt wrapped around His chest. His head and His hair were white like wool, white like snow, and His eyes like a flame of fire. His feet were like polished bronze refined in a furnace, and His voice was like the roar of rushing waters. In His right hand He held seven stars, and out of His mouth came forth a sharp, two-edged sword. His face was like the sun shining at full strength.
>
> When I saw Him, I fell at His feet like a dead man. But He placed His right hand on me, saying, "Do not be afraid! I am the First and the Last, and the One who lives. I was dead, but look—I am alive forever and ever! Moreover, I hold the keys of death and Sheol."
>
> –Revelation 1:13-18, TLV

No man could begin to touch such feet. No man could begin to stand in front of the Anointed One.

The rise of spirits, angels, demons, and devils during the second temple period (516BCE-70CE) is of great interest among scholars, Hellenism being the primary influence. After the Babylonian banishment, more angelic language entered Jewish writings and other spiritual texts. The 3rd century BC started the first day of 300 BCE and is considered part of the Classical era, or historical period when we see a significant rise in these types of angelic figures being categorized:

> The writer of the Book of Daniel was the first by whom angels were individualized and endowed with names and titles. Not long after that time Essenism came into existence. It possessed a highly developed Angelology; but knowledge of the system was confined to Essenes. [7]

The Essenes were a mystical Jewish sect during the 2nd temple period. Today, most are familiar with the Essenes due to the discovery of the Dead Sea Scrolls, thought to be their collection.

According to Cambridge scholar Saul Olyan, author of *A Thousand Thousands Served Him*:

> Exegesis and the Naming of Angels in Ancient Judaism, also points to the Babylonian exile as the pivotal moment after which one finds the "emergence of named angels, classes of heavenly beings, angelic hierarchy, archangels, a complex of heavenly temples and cults, conflicts between good and bad angels, expanding roles of angels in the human sphere, and characterization of angels "within Judaism." [8]

---

[7] https://www.jewishencyclopedia.com/articles/1521-angelology

[8] https://www.cambridge.org/core/journals/ajs-review/article/abs/saul-m-olyan-a-thousand-thousands-served-him-exegesis-and-the-naming-of-

The only place angels are mentioned by name in the Tanakh (Old Testament) is in Daniel Chapters 8-10. In the Talmud, *Yerushalmi | Sefaria,* we find a statement of *Resh Laqish* that the names of the angels brought back from the Babylonian exile were unknown in pre-exilic Israel (*Yerushalmi Rosh haShana* 1:2). However, we do read of angels throughout the Bible, but they mostly remain veiled.

Angels appear to men as human beings transmitting brightness and astonishing beauty. Many times, they are not recognized as angels immediately. At times, the angels are sent to bring punishment. In the Book of Acts, an angel is sent to destroy King Herod:

> Immediately, because Herod did not give glory to God, an angel of the Lord struck him down, and he was eaten by worms and died.
>
> −Acts 12:23, BSB

Paul warns the people of Corinth concerning the Children of Israel who grumbled and complained and mentions a destroying angel sent by the Holy One:

> These things took place as examples to keep us from craving evil things as they did. Do not be idolaters, as

---

angels-in-ancient-judaism-texte-und-studien-zum-antiken-judentum-36-tubingen-j-c-b-mohr-paul-siebeck-1993-xiv-148-pp/376AF2D73147B9D1CDB12C6BD79A4B93 some of them were. As it is written: "The people sat down to eat and to drink and got up to indulge in revelry." We should not commit sexual immorality, as some of them did, and in one day twenty-three thousand of them died. We should not test Christ, as some of them did, and were killed by snakes. And do not complain, as some of them did, and were killed by the destroying angel.

–I Corinthians 10:6-10, BSB

Again, angels do not just bring heavenly messages concerning the Messiah, they also bring death and destruction:

> So *Adonai* sent a pestilence upon Israel from the morning until the appointed time, so that 70,000 men of the people died from Dan to Beersheba. When the angel stretched out his hand toward Jerusalem to destroy it, *Adonai* relented from the calamity and said to the angel who was destroying the people, "Enough! Now withdraw your hand." The angel of *Adonai* was then by the threshing floor of Araunah the Jebusite.

–II Samuel 24:15-16, TLV

Angels, throughout the Bible, fly through the earth and the heavens. Many are described as having wings. Angelic hosts have robes illuminated with light. They disappear in sacrificial fire, and they always obey their Creator, Elohim:

> "Let all God's angels worship Him." Now about the angels

> He says: "He makes His angels winds, His servants flames of fire."
>
> —Hebrews 1:6-7, BSB

> But to which of the angels has He ever said: "Sit at My right hand, Till I make Your enemies Your footstool." Are they not all ministering spirits sent forth to minister for those who will inherit salvation?
>
> —Hebrews 1:13-14, NKJV

When meditating on creation, and the days of creation, the Son of God is described as the first-born over-all creation. This would include the angelic hosts:

> He is the image of the invisible God, the firstborn of all creation. For by Him all things were created—in heaven and on earth, the seen and the unseen, whether thrones or angelic powers or rulers or authorities.
>
> —Colossians 1:15-16, TLV

Other examples include when the soldiers came to arrest Yeshua after Judas had betrayed him with a kiss, we read that twelve legions of angels could come to the Messiah and deliver Him if He wished:

> Do you think that I cannot appeal to my Father, and he will at once send me more than twelve legions of angels?
>
> —Matthew 26:53, ESV

The word legion is a military term equivalent to 6,000 Roman soldiers, although the total number could be higher. When we multiply that number by 12, we get 72,000 angels. The number 72 is curious as the number of the nations is said to be 70 plus Israel and Edom. Moses and Aaron and the 70 elders equals 72, and Yeshua sent 70 elders out to spread the Gospel in Luke 10:1. He sent them out two by two.

Also, King David describes a heavenly host who never disobey Elohim but do only His bidding:

> *Adonai* has set up His throne in the heavens, and His kingdom rules over all. Bless *Adonai*, you angels of His: mighty in strength, performing His word, upon hearing the utterance of His word. Bless *Adonai*, all you His armies, His servants who do His will. Bless *Adonai*, all His works everywhere in His dominion. Bless *Adonai*, O my soul!
>
> –Psalm 103:19-22, TLV

Human-like angels eat heavenly bread (Matzah). Matzah first appears in the Torah in connection with Lot and his unexpected guests. "Now the two angels came to Sodom in the evening, while Lot was sitting at the gate of Sodom" (Genesis 19:1, TLV). Elders sat at the gate. The gate was the place where the socially powerful conducted business. In addition to Lot making them a meal, he baked unleavened bread, which could be prepared fast. "He prepared a feast for them and baked *matzot*, and they ate" Gen. 19:3, TLV). Psalm 78 concerning the children of Israel in the wilderness confirms that unleavened bread is the bread of angels:

> Yet he commanded the skies above and opened the doors of heaven, and he rained down on them manna to eat and gave them the grain of heaven. Man ate of the bread of the angels; he sent them food in abundance.
>
> –Psalm 78:23-25, ESV

The Biblical story of Gideon, who became a judge over Israel involves angels and unleavened cakes as well. After God's people fell into adultery, He turned them over to the Midianites. The people of Israel cried out to the Holy One on account of the Midianites, and the Holy One sent a prophet to the people of Israel. He chastised them for not obeying His voice. Then He sent an angel to speak to his servant Gideon who would lead them to victory with 300 men. The angel majestically vanished before Gideon but not before consuming the offering of meat and unleavened cakes by fire:

> Then the angel of God said to him, "Take the meat and the *matzah* and lay them on this rock, and pour out the broth." So he did so. Then the angel of *Adonai* put out the end of the staff that was in His hand and touched the meat and the *matzah*. Fire sprang up from the rock and

> consumed the meat and the *matzah*. Then the angel of *Adonai* vanished from his sight.
>
> –Judges 6:20-21, TLV

Different types of angels appear to man in human form, displaying brilliant radiance. Some messengers appear as angels, while others are human. The glowing light illuminating these messengers leaves the witnesses in awe. There are multiple terms for these angelic hosts, one being Cherubim. The term Cherubim for angels is seldom used in the Bible except for adorning the tabernacle and its furnishings. The most common word concerning angelic beings is *malak,* meaning messenger. *Malak* is Strong's Hebrew 4397 (messenger). Many heavenly hosts are mentioned in Psalms, Job, and other biblical books. They are described as singing and praising Elohim over all His creation and the works of His hands. The first time we read of these Cherubim is in Genesis after Adam and Eve (*Chavah*) sinned:

> And He drove the man out. And He placed *kerubim* at the east of the garden of Eden, and a flaming sword which turned every way, to guard the way to the tree of life.
>
> –Genesis 3:24, ISR

Brad Scott, author and Hebrew scholar at *WildBranch Ministries,* explains that the cherubim guarded the way to the Tree of Life in his temple teaching *Ark of the Covenant*:

There are to be cherubim at each end of the covering to be of beaten work of pure gold. The verse states that these cherubim are to be *'al-hakapporet* (literally--on) or from the mercy seat. They are to be part of the covering. It is interesting to note that two cherubim were placed at the east of the garden of Eden along with a flaming sword to guard the way of the tree of life (Genesis 3:24). It has been my contention all along that the Torah is the tree of life and that in God's time, took upon flesh and tabernacled among us, and that the New Testament clearly teaches that believing gentiles are made one with this tree. These cherubim were to keep man from access to Torah, in the absence of God's redeeming mercy. For without God's precious grace, Adam or man could live or exist forever in sin without God. Only one man (Messiah) could enter this place. Only that which is perfect could have access. Only one man is worthy. This man, according to God's plan, would begin with a seed. [9]

Envision the mighty angels holding flaming swords to guard the way to the Tree of Life. Only the Holy One holds the power over life and death, and it is He who gives us our very breath. His angels do His bidding, and they are always obedient.

In addition, the Book of Exodus takes great pains to describe the

---

[9] The Tabernacle-4 — The Wild Branch Ministry

golden replicas of the *kerubin* on the Ark of the Covenant:

> Make one cheruv (Cherub) at one end and one cheruv at the other end. Of one piece with the atonement cover you are to make the cheruvim at its two ends. The cheruvim are to spread out their wings above, shielding the atonement cover with their wings, each facing its companion. The faces of the cheruvim are to be turned toward the atonement cover.
>
> –Exodus 25:19-20, TLV

The verse above from Exodus 25 mentions the cherubim's, with their outstretched wings, always facing one another. This picture clarifies Yeshua's words in Matthew 18: "See that you do not despise one of these little ones, for I tell you that their angels in heaven continually see the face of My Father in heaven" (TLV). The earthly tabernacle constructed in the wilderness was a replica of a heavenly tabernacle—on earth as it is in heaven. The Cherubim were placed at the heart of the tabernacle, covering the Ark of the Covenant. This sacred chest is where the commandments were placed, along with the heavenly bread and the staff of Aaron that budded and bloomed. This staff represents our High Priest, Yeshua Messiah. The Messiah explained that these little ones, even the baby lambs, who may not know as much about the Torah, their angels in heaven continually see His Fathers Face.

Not only are these heavenly creatures described as adorning the Ark, but they are also depicted as being embroidered into the curtains of the tabernacle. The veil woven of fine linen, was rent at the death of Yeshua. The linen was blue, crimson, purple, and white, with these cherubim embroidered. The Angelic Cherubim were also embroidered onto the entrance curtain to the Holy Place and the Most Holy Place, the Holy of Holies. However, no Cherubim were embroidered on the outside of the entrance curtain to the Holy Place. The angels were looking into the tabernacle from every angle:

> Moreover, you shall make the tabernacle with ten curtains of fine twined linen and blue and purple and scarlet yarns; you shall make them with cherubim skillfully worked into them. The length of each curtain shall be twenty-eight cubits, and the breadth of each curtain four cubits; all the curtains shall be the same size.
>
> –Exodus 26:1-2, ESV

When Solomon built the temple, he placed the cherubim, palm trees, and flowers throughout:

> And the wings of the cherubim were spread out so that a wing of one touched the one wall, and a wing of the other cherub touched the other wall; their other wings touched each other in the middle of the house. And he overlaid the cherubim with gold. Around all the walls of the house he

carved engraved figures of cherubim and palm trees and open flowers, in the inner and outer rooms. The floor of the house he overlaid with gold in the inner and outer rooms. For the entrance to the inner sanctuary, he made doors of olivewood; the lintel and the doorposts were five-sided. He covered the two doors of olivewood with carvings of cherubim, palm trees, and open flowers. He overlaid them with gold and spread gold on the cherubim and on the palm trees.

–I Kings 6:27-32, ESV

This is a picture of the heavenly replica. The Holy One's throne is seen as sovereign and perched over the Ark of the Covenant-- in heaven as it is on earth:

> The LORD reigns; let the peoples tremble! He sits enthroned upon the cherubim; let the earthquake!
>
> –Psalms 99:1, ESV

The cherubim are closely related to the Seraphim. In Ezekiel 10, the Cherubim are mentioned as having four faces: a face of an ox, a lion, an eagle and a man. The four faces mentioned in Ezekiel 1 and 10 will be covered thoroughly in Part III, Wolves Unseen. Throughout the Bible, we read of these heavenly messengers, but they still remain a mystery. Professor Ellen Muehlberger, assistant professor of Near Eastern Studies and History at the University of Michigan, is quoted in an academic article *The*

History of Angels describing how the characteristics of angels have changed and evolved over time. Frequent topics of debate involved guardian angels and how to get them to do your bidding:

> In late antiquity {the Dark Ages}, the identity of angels was much broader than what it is now: some Christians spoke of Christ as an angel, or suggested that Christian ascetic monks who renounced family, food, drink and sex and lived out in the desert were really angels. But Muehlberger says when the Egyptian monks learned they were being considered angels, they emphatically rejected the idea. [10]

Perhaps the most fascinating description given concerning the cherubim is that Yahweh rides them like a chariot. "He rode upon a *cheruv* and flew" (II Samuel 22:11, TLV). In Psalm 18, David declares that Yahweh soared on the wings of the wind and flew on a cherub to save him from the hand of Saul and all his enemies. David's poetic description evokes a God who is mighty to save. The prophet Ezekiel is quite certain of what he sees in a vision, and it is none other than the Holy One riding upon these winged creatures:

> Then the glory of *Adonai* went forth from above the threshold of the House and stood above

---
[10] The history of angels: U-M research (phys.org)

> the *cheruvim*. The *cheruvim* lifted up their wings and arose from the earth in my sight. When they went out, the wheels went with them. They stood still at the door of the east gate of *Adonai*'s House. The glory of the God of Israel was over them from above. They were the living creatures that I saw under the God of Israel by the river Chebar. I knew that they were *cheruvim*.
>
> –Ezekiel 10:18-20, TLV.

The Holy One is often depicted in the Bible as being shrouded in thick darkness, dark waters, with darkness under His Feet. He flies upon the wings of the wind:

> He bowed the heavens also, and came down: and darkness was under his feet. And he rode upon a cherub, and did fly: yea, he did fly upon the wings of the wind. He made darkness his secret place; his pavilion round about him were dark waters and thick clouds of the skies.
>
> –Psalm 18:9-11, KJV

Spirits Unveiled: Book Two

Chapter 2

ANGELIC HOSTS
PART 2

After becoming deathly sick and losing everything I owned, including my home, I went on a journey of couch surfing. I stayed in many people's homes during this time of pain, loss, and abandonment. My (ex) husband took a job overseas, leaving me vulnerable, too sick to work, and at times too sick to walk. All the suffering was doing a more significant work. I was learning to trust the Holy One for daily bread and provision, and Adonai was always faithful. With the loss of my home, I had to sell my belongings. Some of the greater pains involved my youngest son being displaced and needing to euthanize my cat and dog. My cat had gotten an infection in her eye and became sick and had to be put to rest. My dog, Rex, had become so overprotective of me that he began to bite and growl at anyone who came near me. After taking him to my vet for an evaluation, she said it would be hard to find someone willing to adopt Rex as he had bitten their trained employee hired to work with aggressive animals. My heart was crushed.

Rex had been a beloved pet who laid his head on me and comforted me in my darkest hours, so losing him was exceptionally painful. During this time of heartbreak and physical suffering, I was drawn to the Book of Job, which I read continually. I would imagine the wedding feasts and picture myself seated next to Job, where I could converse with him about pain. I had lost my health, my job, my career, my husband, and my home swiftly. Through this dark whirlwind, I continued to quote Job with tears in my eyes and faith in my belly:

> "Naked I came from my mother's womb,
>
> and naked I will return.
>
> The LORD gave, and the LORD has taken away.
>
> Blessed be the name of the LORD."
>
> In all this, Job did not sin or charge God with wrongdoing.
>
> –Job 1:20-22, BSB

After some time, I regained strength, and the Father placed me in leadership with a pastor in charge of a soup kitchen for the homeless and a group for those struggling with addiction. The pastor and I went to a Christian bookstore one night after a gathering. As we got out of our vehicles, a man approached us. He looked at me and said, "I am not asking for money, but I am hungry. Can you get me some food?" I looked at the man, who appeared to be in his early thirties, and said, "Of course, what would you like?"

"Anything would be so appreciated," he said. "Anything."

I replied, "Well, there is a *Steak and Shake* within walking distance. We will meet you there."

The pastor and I sat at the counter with our new friend Jason and waited for his meal to arrive. I noticed his face appeared strange because it did not look dirty, even though his cheeks were smudged. His face shone with a glow, and his eyes were the bluest eyes I have ever seen. I wanted to know Jason's story. As I inquired, he began to explain his journey. After being laid off from his job, his unemployment benefits ran out before he could find steady work. Later, he said, he became sick and gradually fell behind on his mortgage until he lost his home. He had been living in his car with his beloved cat. One day he said he went to shower and clean up, but while he was away, someone reported his vehicle and had it towed with all his belongings, including his cat. I felt so bad for him and began sharing my story. I was grieved that there were no shelters for single people in the area. Mostly, the nearby shelters were full of mothers with children. I wondered if there were churches helping people in Jason's situation. As I was meditating, Jason looked up at me and said, "You know what I am missing from my car the most?"

I responded, "What?"

He said, "My Bible. I have been studying the Book of Job. Now, there is someone who went through suffering." His eyes twinkled at me, and he said, "You know about Job too, and he has become your friend."

He smiled, and I wondered how he knew I had just told someone that very thing, "Job has become my friend—a friend to help me through my sufferings." Jason referenced scriptures I had been praying, things another human had no way of knowing.

The pastor and I tried to get Jason a motel for the night, but he said he was fine. He pointed across the street and said he was sleeping behind *Best Buy Electronic Store*, where the semi-trucks come in to unload. Jason stated that the manager knew him well and that he would find work soon. We asked if we could pick him up for a service and prayer meeting in the morning, and Jason said yes, that he would be ready and standing outside the *Best Buy* building. We tried to give him money as we parted, but he refused. After praying with Jason and holding his hand, the pastor and I left the restaurant. Once outside, we looked at each other strangely, and I said, "Was Jason an angel?" We looked back at the restaurant, and Jason was gone. The pastor looked to be in awe, "Yes, Bonnie, I think he was an angel." He laughed loudly and his countenance changed to pure joy.

The following day we went to *Best Buy* to pick up Jason, but he was not there. We went inside and asked for the store manager, explaining our talk with Jason and his sleeping there and being homeless. The manager said, "There is no one sleeping out back. I can assure you of that. And I have never heard of him nor seen him. We are back there night and day, going to dumpsters and unloading trucks. I am not sure you have the right store." The pastor and I walked away pondering and meditating on encountering angels unaware. We felt some strange feeling in our souls that was not from this realm as the memory of Jason lingered with us.

Angels are fascinating, and the Bible contains mysterious passages concerning them. An angel of the Lord appears to Abraham, Isaac, and Jacob, and an angel appears twice to Sarah's handmaiden, Hagar. In scripture, some of the writings regarding angels give few clues about their appearances; other writings are strikingly wondrous such as Isaiah's account:

> In the year that King Uzziah died I saw the Lord sitting upon a throne, high and lifted up; and the train of his robe filled the temple. Above him stood the seraphim. Each had six wings: with two he covered his face, and with two he covered his feet, and with two he flew. And one called to another and said:
>
> "Holy, holy, holy is the LORD of hosts; the whole earth is full of his glory!"
>
> –Isaiah 6:1-3, ESV

It is most curious that centuries later, John the revelator, would see these same angelic hosts:

> And in the midst of the throne, and around the throne, *were* four living creatures full of eyes in front and in back. The first living creature *was* like a lion, the second living creature like a calf, the third living creature had a face like a man, and the fourth living creature *was* like a flying eagle. *The* four living creatures, each having six wings, were full of eyes around and within. And they do not rest day or night, saying:
>
> "Holy, holy, holy,
> Lord God Almighty,
> Who was and is and is to come!"
>
> –Revelation 4:6-8, NKJ

According to *Abarim Publications*, the Seraphim, who are known in our culture as handsome human-like angelic creatures, were known to the Hebrews as snake-like fireballs. The word Seraphim means burning and destroyers:

> The other famous scene in which the word *seraphim* is prominently featured deals with the attack of the "fiery serpents" on Israel in the wilderness (Numbers 21:6), which literally reads, "And YHWH sent among the people the *seraphim* serpents." The word for serpent, *nahash*, is related to the words for bronze and the verb to divine, and

the serpent scene of Numbers 21 may be about more than just an animal attack. The serpentine *seraphim* return in Isaiah 14:29, where the prophet foretells the destruction of Philistia, "from the root of the snake (*nahash*) comes a viper (*tzepa*, a word that indicates a snake producing venom), and his fruit (is) a flying *seraph*." Actually, the word "flying" may also mean "dark." See the name Ephah. The flying or dark *seraph* returns in Isaiah 30:6, where it is listed among the beasts of the Negev (desert). [11]

Although, some of these angelic beings cannot be listed under the category of an angel, like the seraphim, with all their mysteries, others seem to take on human form and carry out instructions and bring encouragement to humans. The angels that appear to Abraham's nephew, Lot, appear as humans:

> Now the two angels arrived at Sodom in the evening, and Lot was sitting in the gateway of the city. When Lot saw them, he got up to meet them, bowed facedown, and said, "My lords, please turn aside into the house of your servant; wash your feet and spend the night. Then you can rise early and go on your way.
>
> –Genesis 19:1-2, BSB

In Genesis 37, it could be interpreted that the strange figure of a

---

[11] Seraphim | The amazing word Seraphim: meaning and etymology (abarim-publications.com)

man directing Joseph to his brothers is an angel. Rashi, a medieval French commentator, believed the man to be Gabriel, the angel that appeared to Daniel:

> And a man found him wandering in the fields. And the man asked him, "What are you seeking?" "I am seeking my brothers," he said. "Tell me, please, where they are pasturing the flock." And the man said, "They have gone away, for I heard them say, 'Let us go to Dothan.' So Joseph went after his brothers and found them at Dothan.
>
> –Genesis 37:15-17, ESV

In Exodus, an angel appears to Moses in a burning bush. We learn that angels speak with humans, wrestle with humans, and they can appear as a "satan" or an adversary as we read in Numbers concerning Balaam and his donkey:

> Then the LORD opened Balaam's eyes, and he saw the angel of the LORD standing in the road with a drawn sword in his hand. And Balaam bowed low and fell facedown. The angel of the LORD asked him, "Why have you beaten your donkey these three times? Behold, I have come out to oppose you, because your way is perverse before me. The donkey saw me and turned away from me these three times. If she had not turned away, then by now I would surely have killed you and let her live."
>
> –Numbers 22:31, BSB

Gabriel is an angel who comes to Daniel while in prayer. He is also referred to as a man or a messenger. Gabriel is one of two named angels in the Bible. Michael is the other angel named, and we read that he is an archangel. Gabriel tells Daniel that he has come to bring him insight. Imagine the wonder of a heavenly being speaking and explaining the future:

> "While I was still speaking and praying, confessing my sin and the sin of my people Israel, and presenting my supplication before *Adonai* my God on behalf of the holy mountain of my God— yes, while I was praying, Gabriel, the one I had seen in the earlier vision, came to me swiftly about the time of the evening offering.
>
> "He instructed me and said to me: 'Daniel, I have come now to give you insight and understanding. At the beginning of your requests, a message went out, and I have come to declare it to you, for you are greatly esteemed. Therefore consider the message and understand the vision. . .'"
>
> –Daniel 9:20-23, TLV

In Daniel 8:15, Gabriel appears in the "likeness of man," and in Daniel 9:21, he is mentioned as "the man Gabriel." In Daniel 8:16-17, the prophet Daniel is struck with fear and falls upon his face when he sees this angelic being. Gabriel explains the future concerning the temple, the Messiah, wars, and abomination, giving a direct timeline with dates. Gabriel is an angel who flies from heaven to earth. We also read of the angel Gabriel in the New Testament, as he appears to the father of John the Baptist (immerser) in the temple. Gabriel tells Zechariah that his prayers have been heard, and that his wife Elizabeth will bear a son, and that Zechariah is to name him John (*Yochanan*). Zechariah does not seem to be overly in awe of this angelic being and somewhat suspicious as his wife is old, and he is as well. With great authority, Gabriel tells Zechariah that he stands in the presence of the Holy One:

> "How can I be sure of this?" Zechariah asked the angel. "I am an old man, and my wife is well along in years." "I am Gabriel," replied the angel. "I stand in the presence of God, and I have been sent to speak to you and to bring you this good news. And now you will be silent and unable to speak until the day this comes to pass, because you did not believe my words, which will be fulfilled at their proper time."
>
> –Luke 1:18-20, BSB

This "standing in the presence" is something we read concerning the prophets as well. They stand in His presence to hear His Voice and council before bringing words to the people. The false prophets prophesy out of their own hearts and dream dreams from their own thoughts and do not stand in His authority:

> I did not send these prophets, yet they have run with their message; I did not speak to them, yet they have prophesied. But if they had stood in My council, they would have proclaimed My words to My people and turned them back from their evil ways and deeds.
>
> –Jeremiah 23:21-22, BSB

Angels play a well-designed role as messengers. The Hebrew word *malak*, implies that heavenly Beings, apart from angels, meaning humans, also take messages from Yahweh to His people. Not only does Gabriel come to Elizabeth to bring the good news, but he comes to Miriam (Mary), the mother of Yeshua Messiah, and tells her she has found favor with the Holy One:

> Then in the sixth month, the angel Gabriel was sent by *Adonai* into a town in the Galilee named *Natzeret* and to a virgin engaged to a man named Joseph, of the house of David. The virgin's name was Miriam. And coming to her, the angel said, "*Shalom*, favored one! *Adonai* is with you. But at the message, she was perplexed and kept wondering what kind of greeting this might be. The angel spoke to her, "Do not be afraid, Miriam, for you have found favor with God. Behold, you will become pregnant and give birth to a son, and you shall call His name *Yeshua*.
>
> –Luke 1:26-31, TLV

Angelic beings and prophets were often given insight into things unknown. The Prophets of old were given authority as messengers and were also able to discern secretive things most humans cannot. In II Kings 6, the king of Syria came against Israel to make war. The king consulted his servants and formulated a military tactic to attack, but the prophet Elisha warned the king of Israel and sent word of all the king's plots. The king of Syria was greatly troubled. He called his servants and wanted to know who was leaking their military information. One of his servants tells the king that it is none other than Elisha, the prophet who is in Israel. The servant declares to the king that the prophet Elisha hears the words he speaks from his bedchamber. The king of Syria demands that his servants bring him Elisha. Afterward, a strange fiery awakening happens, and Elisha's servant is given a heavenly view on earth. Is it a vision of a great army of heavenly hosts:

> Therefore he sent horses and chariots and a great army there, and they came by night and surrounded the city. And when the servant of the man of God arose early and went out, there was an army, surrounding the city with horses and chariots. And his servant said to him, "Alas, my master! What shall we do?" So he answered, "Do not fear, for those who are with us are more than those who are with them." And Elisha prayed, and said, "Lord, I pray, open his eyes that he may see." Then the Lord opened the eyes of the young man, and he saw. And

behold, the mountain was full of horses and chariots of fire all around Elisha.

–II Kings 6:15-17, NKJV

The *Book of Maccabees* has a similar story concerning heavenly horses:

When the battle became strong, there appeared out of heaven to their adversaries splendid men on horses with bridles of gold, and two of them, leading on the Jews.

–II Maccabees 10:29

And Psalms 34:7 suggest the same:

The angel of the LORD encamps around those who fear him and delivers them.

–Psalm 34:7, ESV

The patriarch Jacob is sent angels before meeting up with his brother Esau who had wanted to take his life:

Jacob went on his way, and the angels of God met him. And when Jacob saw them he said, "This is God's camp!"

–Genesis 32:1-2, ESV

In Matthew 18, Yeshua professes that guardian angels exist and see the face of His Father:

See that you do not look down on any of these little ones.

> For I tell you that their angels in heaven always see the face of My Father in heaven.
>
> –Matthew 18:10, ESV

The Book of Hebrews implies the same thing: "Are not the angels ministering spirits sent to serve those who will inherit salvation?" (Hebrews 1:14, BSB). In Daniel 6, after Daniel is thrown in a den with hungry lions, at daylight he proclaims an angel came and shut the lions mouths:

> My God sent His angel and shut the mouths of the lions. They have not hurt me, for I was found innocent in His sight, and I have done no wrong against you, O king.
>
> –Daniel 6:22, BSB

The Hebrew Bible is mostly quiet concerning demons and angelic beings placed in a classified order such as in *The Book of Enoch*. The questions to ask are not what these spirits are but why is a grandiose rebellion mostly silent and not of grand importance during the Biblical period until the exile and second temple periods. Hellenism and Greek thought were influencing many. Is Jewish interest shifting during this era due to foreign influence, alienation from Adonai, and falling away from monotheism? We see this swift change concerning *The Book of the Watchers--Enoch*. Most modern scholars estimate the older sections of the *Book (books) of Enoch* date from about 300 BC and the latter portions to the first century BC. This book appears thousands of years after Enoch had lived. Add copying errors over thousands of years with different dated fragments making this Pseudepigrapha literature hard to digest. Pseudepigrapha, meaning falsely credited works, texts whose alleged author is not the genuine author, or a work whose real author attributed it to a figure of the past.

The author of the *Book of Enoch* professes to be Enoch, but this is impossible as the book quotes passages from Isaiah and Daniel. Enoch claims that angels built the ark in I Enoch 67:2. The first Book of the Bible, Genesis, tells us Noah built the ark. The book states that demons taught men to write with paper and ink and that the creation story was told to men by demons. For more on Jude quoting Enoch, read Book I of this series, *Satan Unmasked*. The Book of Enoch teaches a false Messiah. It is easy to get swept up in passages that describe the Messiah and the return of the Messiah because they sound much like the prophets:

> He (Messiah) shall be the hope of those whose hearts are troubled. All, who dwell on earth, shall fall down and worship before him; shall bless and glorify him, and sing praises to the name of the Lord of spirits. In his presence he existed, and has revealed to the saints and to the righteous the wisdom of the Lord of spirits; for he has preserved the lot of the righteous, because they have hated and rejected this world of iniquity, and have

> detested all its works and ways, in the name of the Lord of spirits.[12]
>
> –The Book of Enoch 48:6,7

However, after reading Enoch in its entirety, the messianic Son of Man figure, shown throughout the book, is none other than Enoch. This is not Messiah, Yeshua, the son of Joseph and Miriam. The writer proclaims Enoch to be the Son of God. Books like Enoch are great for historians and researchers. This way, we can see how angels, demons, and different dogmas evolved, but many can be led astray without careful study.

Mystical language in the number of stories concerning angelic hosts in the Bible leaves many unanswered questions. Angels strike men with death, pestilence, and war. However, they also guard with flaming swords and bring warnings and protection to the righteous. They announce the births of the Messiah, John the Baptist, and Samson, among others, and they are always exalting in praise around the throne of Yahweh to give Him glory:

> The four living creatures, each having six wings, were full of eyes all around and within. They do not rest day or night, chanting,
>
> *"Kadosh, kadosh, kadosh*
>   *Adonai Elohei-Tzva'ot,*

---
[12] Chapter 48 [1] – The Book of Enoch (book-ofenoch.com)

asher haya v'hoveh v'yavo!
Holy, holy, holy
   is the Lord God of Hosts,
   who was and who is
   and who is to come!"

And whenever the living creatures give glory and honor and thanks to the One seated on the throne, who lives forever and ever.

–Revelation 4:8-9, TLV

Concerning angelic beings, there is much to meditate on. Angels are given assignments from the Holy One. They are powerful, fearful, and full of glorious wisdom and light. They are beyond our full scope of comprehension and remain shrouded in mystery.

Chapter 3

Dry Places

Exorcisms have made Hollywood considerable money. Multiple movies and even television shows depict demons, death, and necromancy. Numerous books and teachings have been written about demons. All the main religions of the world have a formula for expelling demons. In Matthew 12, Yeshua heals a man who has a withered hand. Shortly after this miracle, He heals a man oppressed, blind, and mute. "Then a demon-oppressed man who was blind and mute was brought to him, and he healed him, so that the man spoke and saw" (Matthew 12:22, TLV). Afterward, Yeshua is harshly insulted by the Pharisees:

> Then a demon-plagued man, who was blind and mute, was brought to *Yeshua*; and He healed him, so that he spoke and saw. All the crowds were astounded and saying, "This can't be *Ben-David*, can it?"
>
> But hearing this, the Pharisees said, "This fellow drives out demons only by beelzebul, the ruler of demons."
>
> –Matthew 12:22-24, TLV

The title *Beelzebub* means Lord of the flies and comes from Baal, the male god of Canaan, and the Phoenicians, the counterpart of the female Asherah. After the religious leaders accuse Yeshua of performing miracles by Beelzebub, He tells the leaders that anyone who speaks against the Son of God may be forgiven. Still, this blasphemy against the Spirit that hovered over the waters in Genesis 1, the Holy Spirit (*Ruach HaKodesh*) would not be forgiven. Yeshua continues by presenting the Pharisees and Sadducees with a question: "If Satan drives out Satan, he is divided against himself. How then can his kingdom stand?" (Matthew 12:26, BSB). Shortly after this rebuttal, Yeshua presents an allegory of a man whose condition becomes worse after seven spirits enter him:

> Now when the unclean spirit goes out of a man, it passes through waterless places seeking rest, and does not find it. Then it says, "I will return to my house from which I came;" and when it comes, it finds it unoccupied, swept, and put in order. Then it goes and takes along with it seven other spirits more wicked than itself, and they go in and live there; and the last state of that man becomes worse than the first. That is the way it will also be with this evil generation.
>
> –Matthew 12:43-45, NASB

Author and teacher, Kisha Gallagher at *Grace in Torah Website* describes the Hebrew number 7:

(Shvah) Rest, wholeness, completeness, being ripe, order, stability, and holiness. Also, the number of the Temple, Adonai's House. We rest (7) in the finished work (6) of the Messiah. There are seven days of creation, seven days for Temple dedication, seven Spirits of God, seven feasts of God, seven churches or assemblies in Revelation, seven stars in Yeshua's hand, seven golden lampstands, seven seals, seven trumpets, seven bowls, seven thunders that speak, seven eyes of the Lord, seven horns & eyes on the Lamb, seven abominations (wicked lamp spirits Pr. 6:16-19).

Gallagher references *The Creation Gospel: Workbook Two*, a teaching by author and scholar Dr. Hollisa Alewine, *The Seven Abominations of the Wicked Lamp*. In this study, Alewine goes over the seven abominations listed in Proverbs 6. These are opposite from the righteous lamp of the Menorah. In Matthew 12, Yeshua is referring to the seven spirits listed in Proverbs 6:

> There are six things that the LORD hates, seven that are an abomination to him: haughty eyes, a lying tongue, and hands that shed innocent blood, a heart that devises wicked plans, feet that make haste to run to evil, a false witness who breathes out lies, and one who sows discord among brothers.
>
> –Proverbs 6:16-19, ESV

To repeat, the seven abominations are:

1. Haughty eyes (pride)

2. A lying tongue

3. Hands that shed blood (slander/gossip/murder)

4. Wicked plans

5. Feet walking in unrighteousness

6. False witness (Jezebel)

7. One who sows discord among brothers

Allegorically, the demon possessed man that was blind and mute, which Yeshua healed in Matthew 12, represents the condition of some of the corrupt leadership in control of the temple, His Father's House. Remember the number seven in Hebrew represents the temple. The leaders had become blind to their condition. They were like one mute, unable to speak with power and authority, and possessed with pride.

Why would Yeshua bring this message after the accusations concerning Him casting out demons by Beelzebub, Lord of the flies? The Leaders have committed possibly every one of the sins listed by blaspheming the *Ruach HaKodesh* (Holy Spirit). Through their pride, they have accused Yeshua falsely, slandered Him, spoken lies against His character, and caused discord among the people.

The seven abominations listed in Proverbs 6 may reveal what Yeshua references in Mathew 12:43. These unclean spirits would describe our fleshly nature at its worst. The house was clean and swept, and the spirit traveled through waterless places. This dry, arid condition needs to be filled with living water.

Yeshua compares the leaders to an evil generation who call evil good and good evil. The Pharisees and Scribes had seen His mighty miracles and witnessed the Father's power working through Him, and yet, they blasphemed and gave credit to Beelzebub. Astonishingly, blind eyes were just opened in front of them, and a mute man was now speaking and more than likely praising God. The Scholars compared the Messiah's miracles to a pile of dung:

> Ba'al Zəbûb (Beelzebub) is variously understood to mean "lord of the flies" or "lord of the (heavenly) dwelling." Jewish scholars have interpreted the title of "Lord of Flies" as the Hebrew way of calling Ba'al a pile of dung and comparing Ba'al followers to flies. [13]

The religious rulers who stood in front of the Messiah thought their houses (temples) were in order—swept and clean. They were in political places of power. However, they lacked the spirit of humility and grace. Their Temple was standing adorned in all its glory, but Yeshua warns them that not one stone would be left

---

[13] https://www.liquisearch.com/beezlebub/hebrew_bible

upon another (70 AD). This passage from Matthew 12 may be less about demonic spirits and more about the Messiah's own people not accepting or seeing that He was truly the Anointed One. Deliverance and casting out demons will do little good if the person does not believe that Yeshua is the Messiah--the Word made flesh. It is Adonai's Word, His Spirit, and Truth that washes us clean. His Word is like a scented bar of soap if we are obedient and do what it says. Yeshua is the one that brings water in dry places, as He is living water.

Zechariah 14 suggests that during the millennial reign, certain people will have no rain on their land. These people and nations are said to be in a dry place:

> And it will be that whichever of the families of the earth does not go up to Jerusalem to worship the King, the LORD of hosts, there will be no rain on them. If the family of Egypt does not go up or enter, then no rain will fall on them; it will be the plague with которой the LORD smites the nations who do not go up to celebrate the Feast of Booths. This will be the punishment of Egypt, and the punishment of all the nations who do not go up to celebrate the Feast of Booths.
>
> –Zechariah 14:16-19, NASB

Rain does not just happen in the natural, but it also represents the spiritual. When we have no rain, we are in a dry place. It is hard to bear much fruit when there is no rain or refreshment. Another clue to this rain is found in the Torah and compares the Lord's Word to sweet rain:

> Give ear, O heavens, and I will speak, and let the earth hear the words of my mouth. May my teaching drop as the rain, my speech distill as the dew, like gentle rain upon the tender grass, and like showers upon the herb.
>
> —Deuteronomy 32:1-2, ESV

Moses's words in Deuteronomy evoke beautiful imagery. One greater than Moses is here. One greater than Moses was performing many miracles and bringing many corrections in Matthew 12. Fear of demonic spirits is far from the main point of the parable Yeshua shared concerning seven spirits. The heart of the matter is usually a matter of the heart. If Satan casts out Satan, he is divided against himself. Keeping our temples clean and our lamps burning with fresh oil is essential. No one wants a dry, empty house where seven more spirits can enter and make us unclean and worse than we were before.

Spirits Unveiled: Book Two

Chapter 4

A Herd of Pigs

In Luke 8, Yeshua and his disciples take a boat ride to Gerasene to heal men living in death. In the Gospel of Matthew, we read Gadarenes. In Mark, it is the land of the Gerasenes. This location may have been the land of Geshur (Joshua 13:13) in ancient times, but scholars have various opinions. Multiple questions arise when studying this story:

> Then they sailed to the country of the Gerasenes, which is opposite Galilee. And when He [Yeshua] stepped out onto the land, a man from the city met Him who was possessed with demons; and he had not put on clothing for a long time and was not living in a house, but among the tombs. And seeing Jesus, he cried out and fell down before Him, and said with a loud voice, "What business do You have with me, Jesus, Son of the Most High God?"
>
> –Luke 8:26-28, ESV

The passage above says the man had not put on clothing for a long time. The Torah/commandments and instructions for a blessed life are considered clothing. Adam and Eve broke the commandments and realized they were naked. Job said, "I put on righteousness, and it clothed me; my justice was like a robe and a turban" (Job 29:14, ESV). "Behold, I am coming like a thief! Blessed is the one who stays awake, keeping his garments on, that he may not go about naked and be seen exposed!" (Revelation 16:15, ESV). Again, multiple passages confirm spiritual clothing:

> I will greatly rejoice in the Lord; my soul shall exult in my God, for he has clothed me with the garments of salvation; he has covered me with the robe of righteousness, as a bridegroom decks himself like a priest with a beautiful headdress, and as a bride adorns herself with her jewels.
>
> –Isaiah 61:10, ESV

However, harsh taskmasters and rulers can cause many to become naked by poverty and injustice.

This demonized man knows precisely who Yeshua is. He calls Him Yeshua, Son of the Most High God. The demons inside this man fear the Son of Elohim. The Bible says the demons believe and tremble (James 2:19):

> Seeing *Yeshua*, he cried out and fell down before *Yeshua*, and with a loud voice said, "What's between You and me, *Yeshua, Ben El Elyon*? I'm begging You, do not torment me!" For *Yeshua* commanded the defiling spirit

> to come out of the man. For many times it had seized him so that, even though he was restrained and bound with chains and shackles, he would break the chains and be driven by the demons into the desert.
>
> *Yeshua* questioned him, "What is your name?"
>
> "Legion," he said, for many demons had entered him. They kept begging Him not to command them to depart into the abyss.
>
> –Luke 8:28-31, TLV

The Messiah commanded the defiling spirit to come out, but at first, it did not seem to budge but instead spoke through the man. Yeshua then asked the man, "What is your name? Legion, he said." Interestingly, in Luke 8:29, the demon is singular and referred to as a "defiling spirit." Still, as we move along in the story, we learn that there were many unclean spirits tormenting the man. The Messiah gives the demons permission to go into pigs, a herd of swine instead of going to the abyss. The abyss is the home of the dead and evil spirits:

> Now a large herd of pigs was feeding on the mountain. The demons urged *Yeshua* to let them enter these pigs, and He gave them permission. Then the demons came out of the man and entered into the pigs. The herd rushed down the cliff into the lake and was drowned.
>
> –Luke 8:32-33, TLV

Where did the herd of drowned pigs go, if not the abyss?

I once prayed for a man who had come to my home for a ministry gathering. As we prayed for him, he began to throw up repeatedly. He continued to be prayed for and anointed with oil. Later that evening, after everyone had left, I sat on the couch to relax, and across the room, in the far corner, the glass globe of my brass pole lamp flew and shattered on the coffee table in front of me. Glass was everywhere, including on me. I was startled by this. After cleaning up the mess a while later, my cat Jada began to purr at the front door for me to let her outside. Jada was seven years old and a lovely companion. Although she was more introverted, she had never harmed us. I had another cat, a tabby. He was fat and happy and very affectionate. A while later, Jada was purring again to be let back inside the house. It was a daily action, repeated for years, that went smoothly. Jada purred; we opened the door. This night as soon as I opened the door, she lept on me and began clawing and biting my legs. The tabby started to bite me as well. It was as if they were in a frenzy.

I was hysterical and finally grabbed a large candle holder, knocked them off, grabbed my car keys, and fled my house. I was so shaken I went to my then 16-year-old son's job at Subway. He said, "Mom what are you doing here?" I said, "I need you to come home now and put the cats in cages." "He, said mom, you know I can't leave, I have to close the store." I pulled my pant legs up and showed him my bloody legs, and he was in disbelief. That night, with gloves, he was able to get the cats in cages. The next day Jada was her old self, but I was still leery of her. Did the demons go into my cats? Only God knows.

Abarim Publications has an interesting definition for the word *legion*:

> By stating that his name is Legion, the demoniac is being quite specific. In modern English we like to use the word legion to indicate a myriad, but that's not what the word legion meant to the people of the first century AD. Back in the day, the word legion was a Roman-specific term, much like "SS" was to the Nazis or "Stasi" was to East Germany. By using the word legion (instead of calling himself, say, Ten Cohorts) the demoniac makes a point to indicate that his demonic infection consists of "Roman citizens." He is Israel and his demonic infection is the Roman occupation. [14]

The Romans were cruel taskmasters. The Romans taxed the people heavily, and if they refused, they publicly made a spectacle of them by crucifying anyone who did not obey. Crucifixion was perfected by the Romans. Regardless of where or how the infection came about, this man at the tombs was mentally tormented and needed relief. The demons are begging to go into swine. The man who says, "Legion," is not alone at the

---

[14] https://www.abarim-publications.com/Meaning/Legion.html

tombs. Although some passages in the Gospels refer to one man living at the tombs, we read in Matthew 8 that there were two:

> And when he came to the other side, to the country of the Gadarenes, two demon-possessed men met him, coming out of the tombs, so fierce that no one could pass that way.
>
> –Matthew 8:28, ESV

Swine are listed in the Bible as animals unclean for consumption. Pigs or hogs were created like other animals mentioned in Deuteronomy 14 and Leviticus 11 to clean up waste just as a vulture would. However, the Romans sacrificed the pigs to their many gods. In Matthew 8, the demons beg to go to an unclean place. Pigs do not like clean temples:

> The herd rushed down the cliff into the lake and was drowned. But when the herdsmen saw what happened, they ran away and reported it in the town and countryside. People went out to see what had happened. They came to *Yeshua* and found the man from whom the demons had gone—clothed and in his right mind, sitting at the feet of *Yeshua*. And they were frightened.
>
> –Luke 8:33-35, TLV

The Messiah had taken a boat ride to the tombs on purpose. He was on assignment. Before He and his disciples arrive at Gerasene's, a storm begins to rage at sea:

> Then as they were sailing, He {Yeshua} fell asleep. A violent windstorm came down on the lake, and they were swamped with water and in danger.
>
> They came to *Yeshua* and woke Him, saying, "Master, Master, we're perishing!" He got up and rebuked the wind and the surging wave of water. Then they stopped, and it became calm.
>
> –Luke 8:23-24, TLV

The authority of the Messiah is unfathomable. He told the wind and the waves to obey Him, and they did. He told the demons tormenting the man, to Go! And they did.

After the men are set free and changed, something peculiar happens. The townspeople see the men clothed in their right minds and set free. Instead of getting excited about the two men's transformations and the power of the Messiah, they become terrified and plead with Yeshua to leave:

> And all the people from the region surrounding the Gerasenes asked *Yeshua* to go away from them because they were overcome by great fear. So He got into a boat and returned.
>
> –Luke 8:37, TLV

Men are frightened when they see the power of something that transformative. A man chained, cutting himself, naked and without clothing, living in the place of death is a horrific sight. A man who is clean, dressed, and in his right mind is a spectacle for the world. The presence of this man's face shining before them caused them to realize they, too, needed a savior, clothing, and salvation. They feared the power of the Holy Spirit (Ruach HaKodesh).

The man with the legion of demons at the tombs is a prime example of deliverance at its best. He was living among the dead. He was in a place of darkness, dark thoughts (oppression), naked (without spiritual clothing), cutting himself (trauma), and crying out. When we compare this story with the man in Luke 11 whose house was clean, swept, and empty, in which seven more spirits came and worsened his condition, multiple questions arise. In Luke 8, the demons urged *Yeshua* to let them enter the pigs, and He permitted the demons. Why would the demons at the tombs beg and plead to enter pigs if they could take more demons and return to this man's house (temple)? The demons speaking through the man at the tombs would not entreat and plead to go in pigs if they could return and reenter this man again (Luke 8:32). Messiah Yeshua had the power to send these spirits to the pit. Still, the herd of swine depicts the uncleanliness of a person before they are spiritually changed. Yeshua warns, "Do not give what is holy to the dogs; nor cast your pearls before swine, lest they trample them under their feet, and turn and tear you in pieces" (Matthew 7:6, NKJ). Those who reject the Messiah and turn back to sin after being set free and delivered are compared to a sow in II Peter 2, "For it would have been better for them not to have known the way of righteousness, than after learning about it, to turn back from the holy commandment passed on to them. What has happened to them confirms the truth of the proverb, "A dog returns to its vomit," and "A scrubbed pig heads right back into the mud" (II Peter 2:21-22, TLV).

In Luke 15, we read about two sons. One son represents the House of Judah. The other son describes the House of Israel, to whom the Father issued a certificate of divorce and scattered them throughout the earth. As mentioned earlier, the younger son comes to his senses in a pigsty:

> Not many days later, the younger son gathered all he had and took a journey into a far country, and there he squandered his property in reckless living. And when he had spent everything, a severe famine arose in that country, and he began to be in need. So he went and hired himself out to one of the citizens of that country, who sent him into his fields to feed pigs. And he was longing to be fed with the pods that the pigs ate, and no one gave him anything. But when he came to himself, he said, 'How many of my father's hired servants have more than enough bread, but I perish here with hunger! I will arise and go to my father, and I will say to him, "Father, I have sinned against heaven and before you."
>
> –Luke 15:13-18, ESV

The condition of the men at the tombs was severe. Yeshua was making a statement concerning what causes this type of condition and sent the spirits to a proper home, a herd of swine. Over time, many stories about spirits have brought fear and angst. Uncovering and defining the spirits as something different than the world brings compassion and empathy for those who are suffering, chained in bondage, broken, struggling with mental health issues, addiction, and so forth, instead of a demonized person who is evil and needs holy water, a large cross, or an exorcist. The world needs the power of the Holy Spirit and compassion:

> Then the seventy returned with joy, saying, "Master, even the demons submit to us in Your name!" And *Yeshua* said to them, "I was watching satan fall like lightning from heaven. Behold, I have given you authority to trample upon serpents and scorpions, and over all the power of the enemy; nothing will harm you. Nevertheless, do not rejoice that the spirits submit to you, but rejoice that your names have been written in the heavens.
>
> –Luke 10:17-20, TLV

Spirits Unveiled: Book Two

Chapter 5

POSSESSION AND DELIVERANCE

The spirit world is full of intriguing mystery—warring spirits and spirits of light, both given direct orders from the God of Israel. II Kings 19, speaks of the king of Assyria, who had taken over and conquered a large majority of the territory. This evil tyrant is now bent on taking over Israel, but after a humble prayer from King Hezekiah, an army of 180,000 soldiers are slain by an angel of the Lord:

> Then it came about that night that the angel of *Adonai* went out and struck down 185,000 men in the Assyrian camp. When the men arose early in the morning, behold, they were all dead corpses. So King Sennacherib of Assyria withdrew, went away, and returned home, and stayed in Nineveh.
>
> –II Kings 19:35-36, TLV

Who is this Angel of the Lord in II Kings and other passages? Could it be the Messiah? The Father sends famine, war, and He sends angelic beings, but what about the demons that lurk? What about the possession of demons and a legion of demons? Most of us have experienced some form of unease, whether it was doors that shut on their own or objects that move in front of our faces, but what of those tormented souls making guttural sounds with strength like Samson? In today's world, we rely on science to explain much of what we do not understand, and most of the time, science is fairly accurate. Although different mental health issues exist and with medication can be treated, such as depression, schizophrenia, and Bi-Polar disorder, we still have unexplainable cases that point to demonic possession. Many medical experts are left baffled by unexplainable mental symptoms in our present age. Today, psychiatrists and psychologists have diagnosed persons that can only be described in their expert opinion as "possessed."

Dr. M. Scott Peck (1936-2005) wrote *People of the Lie and Glimpses of the Devil*. Matt Herndon in his blog titled *People of the Lie* gives an inside look at Dr. Scott Peck and his thoughts concerning possession. Peck was a psychiatrist who taught at Case Western Reserve. He became convinced that demonic possession is a reality but noting that not all wrongdoers are seized by demons. In his book, Dr. Peck describes experiences with clients whom he sincerely believed were possessed. He was invited to work with a team of caregivers, priests, and psychologists to observe exorcisms on these oppressed people. Dr. Peck longed for healing for these troubled souls.

According to Herndon, Dr. Scott Peck writes that Psychiatrist of various sorts are powerless to help the oppressed unless they know what they're dealing with and are prepared to face it. In his experience, once a diagnosis of evil is made, the caregiver must gird their loins and be prepared to address the spirits forcefully. Battling evil is more often than not a battle of power and will. Insightfully, Peck notes the comparison he sees in Jesus' battles—and they were *battles*—with demonically oppressed persons in the gospels. Jesus didn't try talking therapy with these people. Using his authority—which the demons somehow recognized—he lovingly but forcefully ordered them freed. [15]

The Gospel of Luke includes an account where the demons in one man spoke through his host to Yeshua directly:

> And in the synagogue, there was a man who had the spirit of an unclean demon, and he cried out with a loud voice, "Ha! What have you to do with us, Jesus of Nazareth? Have you come to destroy us? I know who you are—the Holy One of God." But Jesus rebuked him, saying, "Be silent and come out of him!" And when the demon had thrown him down in their midst, he came out of him, having done him no harm. And they were all amazed and

---

[15] "People of the Lie" by M. Scott Peck — smatterings.net

> said to one another, "What is this word? For with authority and power he commands the unclean spirits, and they come out!" And reports about him went out into every place in the surrounding region.
>
> –Luke 4:33-37, ESV

Yeshua did not use burning incense, or artifacts such as crosses to exorcize demons. Yeshua did not use an ancient prayer or incantations. Yeshua commanded the demons to leave, and they did.

Accounts of possessions of demons are given throughout the New Testament, and one woman in the Book of Acts had a python spirit:

> As we were going to the place of prayer, we were met by a slave girl who had a spirit of divination and brought her owners much gain by fortune-telling. She followed Paul and us, crying out, "These men are servants of the Most High God, who proclaim to you the way of salvation." And this she kept doing for many days. Paul, having become greatly annoyed, turned and said to the spirit, "I command you in the name of Jesus Christ to come out of her." And it came out that very hour.
>
> –Acts 16:16-18, ESV

Here, the word divination is clairvoyance from Strong's Greek 4436, a Python, i.e., inspiration. Her words declared the truth.

She insisted that the apostles are servants of the Holy One, but the Apostle Paul was aware of the underlying spirit hidden in this woman.

While working in deliverance ministry, I witnessed all types of oppressive situations, including tormented people. Some were oppressed by spirits, others by pharmaceutical drugs. One example was a happy and healthy person placed on a prescription to treat shingles. Weeks went by and this person's behavior became erratic. And after hearing voices prompting the patient to commit suicide, the person confided in their spouse, who looked up the side effects of the medication and found the number one side effect was suicidal thoughts. Not only that, but several lawsuits had been taken out against this drug company by loved ones whose family members had killed themselves. Once the patients were taken off the medication, their thoughts cleared, and they soon were back to their old selves. However, not all patients experienced this reaction to that drug. On the flip side, I have heard pastors encourage patients to stop taking their medications or known of patients who quit on their own and watched in horror at the repercussions.

Long before Yeshua walked the earth and commanded demons to flee with instant results, men tried to bring deliverance on their own through trial and error. During the Babylonian exile 586 BCE, an increase of seeing angels and demons in Israelite theology and writings began to flourish.

Following the destruction of the Jewish temple, Judaism emerged. Even though the Torah makes little reference to the supernatural, the Babylonian Talmud deals with it at great length. It even gives magical incantations on how to rid these entities. However, the Jerusalem Talmud hardly mentions these demons. The Jerusalem Talmud predates the Babylonian Talmud by around 200 years. Exorcism is absent mostly in rabbinical literature, but the Babylonian Talmud goes into extensive detail. The following passages are complex and somewhat troubling to read:

> Demons were created in the era of Adam. Until the age of 130, Adam was separated from his wife because of his sins, and from the drops of his ejaculate were formed demons, spirits, and lilin (with the form of man and with wings) (Eruvin 18b).

The Babylonian Talmud states some of the people in the generation of the flood of Noah turned into demons. The Talmud gives a recipe to see a demon:

> They cannot be seen by the naked eye; to see them, one must take the placenta of a black cat, daughter of a black cat, firstborn daughter of a firstborn, and burn it to ashes. Put the ashes in one's eyes, and then one can see the demons. (Berachot) 6a. [16]

---
[16] Magic in the Talmud | Daat Emet

By the first century, the religious culture of Israel had nearly 400 years of Hellenized practice. Other strange, suggested remedies was well-sifted dust around one's bed at night. The flour was said to reveal the signs of demon and will leave markings of chicken feet in the dust.

> The Jerusalem Talmud and its rabbis all but reject the possibility of the existence of demons. You can also take comfort in what Maimonides, the Rambam, has to say on the issue: "Belief in astrology, sorcery, oaths, lucky charms, demons, forecasting the future, and talking to the dead – all these are the essence of idol worship, and are lies.... He who believes in these is nothing but a fool." [17]

Whether Rambam, a medieval Sephardic Jewish philosopher, believes in demons or demon possession, many do. Numerous cases of demonic oppression and possession have been backed by ministers, witnesses, psychologists, and medical doctors.

In another experience, while in deliverance ministry, I witnessed people coming for help who were depressed, suicidal, and mentally ill, oppressed, and, yes, possessed. One woman stands out more than most, possibly because my husband helped minister to the woman with me. This was the first time I met who was to be my future husband. The lady tormented by demons attended weekly meetings with her child. I was the newly

---

[17] Judaism and Demons: Does the Torah Address the Occult? | United with Israel

appointed Prayer Director. The spirits in the woman bothered me, and the Holy Spirit in me seemed to bother her. The woman was in her late 30's or early 40's. She dyed her hair black and wore contacts that made her eyes appear gothic or without pupils. Each finger was encased with a skull ring or some demonic-looking adornment, including a pentagram. She laughed mockingly at all the wrong times, and she wore a choker around her neck with a substantial grotesque-looking skull. Her attire was something you might see at a rock concert or a Satanist event. The woman was friendly with many. She mingled and even complimented the pastors' messages but always made sure to tell him how much she disliked the adult class I taught.

A few weeks later, unbeknownst to me, my future husband and an evangelist from South Africa showed up to speak and then afterward offer prayers. After the message, a steady line of people came forward for prayer, including this woman. I began praying that she would get delivered. As she began to request prayer for a family member, the evangelist and my husband started to lay hands on her and pray. Soon she was shrieking on the floor and convulsing. They raised her up and prayed and commanded every demonic spirit to flee in the Name of Yeshua Messiah. The woman stopped screaming and growling, slumped down, and became quiet. Soon she was praising the Father and crying tears of joy. I was so blessed to see this transformation, but I knew it was incomplete.

The following week, the woman came, and she had no contact lenses in and no thick black eye makeup. Her hair was softer, and her skull rings were utterly gone—well, all but one. She still had on dark clothing. I looked at her neck, and the huge skull was still wrapped in a black velvet choker style necklace. As always, prayer was offered at the end of the service for anyone who wanted to come down front. Although several people on the prayer team stood down at the front, she got in my line. As I prayed with her, I told her the Holy One wanted her to remove the skeleton necklace. She no longer walked in death but life. I explained that the skull was choking her walk. Anger flared up in her eyes, and sparks flew. "I am not getting rid of my necklace. This is my favorite necklace," she screamed! "And who are you to judge me?" I calmly informed her I was not judging her and that I too had to get delivered from many things along my journey. "You are a child of light now, not darkness," I told her quoting scripture. I then anointed her with oil and prayed over her. The following week she came in the assembly and made a beeline to me. "I removed my choker," she said. Her eyes were bright, and she had on a bright floral top. She hugged me and thanked me for praying. Each week she shared something that insinuated she was healing and removing things from her life that she knew was not a representative of a child of the Kingdom of Messiah. From this illustration, my point is not all deliverance is instantaneous, and we all must work on our salvation. The Father desires obedience. At times, the adversary comes as an angel of light, and sometimes we mistake darkness for light. Healing from our past takes courage, obedience to the Father's Word, and at times, it takes persistence and counsel. The Holy One wants to see all His children set free and delivered:

> Therefore do not become partners with them; for at one time you were darkness, but now you are light in the Lord. Walk as children of light (for the fruit of light is found in all that is good and right and true), and try to discern what is pleasing to the Lord. Take no part in the unfruitful works of darkness but instead expose them. For it is shameful even to speak of the things that they do in secret. But when anything is exposed by the light, it becomes visible, for anything that becomes visible is light.
>
> –Ephesians 5:7-14, ESV

We are to walk in the light and stay close to our Master Yeshua. The demonic realm is full of darkness, but the Light of the world has come, and He lives in all blood-bought believers and can deliver us from the darkness of this world and bring us into His marvelous light.

Spirits Unveiled: Book Two

Chapter 6

HEAVENLY AGENTS

I will never forget receiving a call from a pastor years ago. His voice was urgent; he needed me to drive over to the congregation as soon as possible. A woman in torment was on her way. She was accompanied by her husband, and the pastor requested my help to pray over her. I remember feeling so helpless and so inadequate. I told the Father on the way there that He would have to take over. Yes, He would have to give me discernment and wisdom concerning this woman. Deliverance ministry leadership was something new I had been plunged into of late.

I can still picture the woman's face and her tears. She seemed so fearful. Her body was shaking as she told me stories of how she could not say the name of our Messiah. I listened as she tried to enunciate each syllable, and her eyes were wildly twitching. I wondered if she had mental issues. The lady informed me that she had wanted to read her Bible the night before but couldn't speak the words. She felt as if something was choking her and controlling her. Her sleep was interrupted by nightmares, awakening with her body paralyzed, and what she referred to as being strangled in her sleep. There were bruises on her arms and places that looked red. After praying over her, the pastor left the room to get some paperwork for her to fill out. In that second, the Holy Spirit quickened me, "Tekoa, take her hand and cast out the spirit of death." I immediately did what I was instructed to do. As I prayed, I did not feel anything or understand what if anything was happening, but I prayed with authority in the name of Yeshua and placed my hands on her head.

The following day the woman called me on the phone. This was not uncommon for making appointments for counsel. She said, "Tekoa, I know that you are unaware of this, but I have been contemplating suicide for months. I had it all planned out. I even bought a dress to be buried in. It's hanging in my closet. I have cut my wrist repeatedly, and I have a bottle of sleeping pills by my bed. I planned on taking them all. Every night for months, I have been tormented and cannot sleep, but last night, after you prayed for me yesterday, I had the most peaceful sleep. I cannot remember the last time this happened. I have no desire now to take my life. Tekoa, I want to live." As she continued, her voice, elated with new hope, brought me to tears. She, too, was crying, only this time it was tears of joy. I was so humbled the Holy One had used me to minister to her.

After my experience with the woman and dealing with a

spirit of death, I became strangely interested in the word "spirit or spirits," especially in the Old Testament. In I Kings 22, King Ahab is preparing to go to war with Aram. The King inquires of the official prophets about the possibility of success. All the prophets told him he would be triumphant in battle, except Micaiah. According to scripture, a lying spirit had enticed the other prophets. Ahab does not want to inquire of Micaiah because he never prophesies anything good to him. After being pressed by Jehoshaphat, he calls for the true prophet of the Holy One, and Micaiah brings a most peculiar warning:

> And Micaiah said, "Therefore hear the word of the LORD: I saw the LORD sitting on his throne, and all the host of heaven standing beside him on his right hand and on his left; and the LORD said, "Who will entice Ahab, that he may go up and fall at Ramoth-gilead?" And one said one thing, and another said another. Then a spirit came forward and stood before the LORD, saying, "I will entice him." And the LORD said to him, "By what means?" And he said, "I will go out, and will be a lying spirit in the mouth of all his prophets." And he said, "You are to entice him, and you shall succeed; go out and do so." Now therefore behold, the LORD has put a lying spirit in the mouth of all these your prophets; the LORD has declared disaster for you.
>
> –I Kings 22:19-23, ESV

Micaiah revealed the truth to Ahab. He even warned the king how he would be enticed by the lying false prophets so that Ahab would go into battle and be defeated. The Book of Ezekiel has a similar passage for those who have taken idols into their hearts and have been led astray:

> And if the prophet be deceived when he hath spoken a thing, I the Lord have deceived that prophet, and I will stretch out my hand upon him, and will destroy him from the midst of my people Israel.
>
> –Ezekiel 14:9, KJV

Deception is something we do not picture a loving God doing. Did the Holy One deceive Ahab so he would go to war and lose his life? Yes, Adonai did. Many times, we forget that it was the Lord who sent the plagues on Egypt by angels. Strong's 4397 is *Malak* and is the word for messenger. This word, translated as an angel, represents both human and spiritual, as in the form of angels. Most of the time, when the Hebrew word *mal'lakh*, or the Greek word *aggelos*, is used, they refer to human messengers. "He cast upon them the fierceness of his anger, wrath, and indignation, and trouble, by sending evil (destroying) angels among them" (Psalm 78:49, KJV). Not only do we read about lying spirits or angelic beings sent to destroy, we learn of tormenting spirits, and they are not sent from Satan but by the Holy One:

> But the spirit of the Father departed from Saul, and an evil spirit from the Father troubled him. And Saul's servants said unto him, Behold now, an evil spirit from God troubleth thee.
>
> —I Samuel 16:14-15, KJV

> And it came to pass, when the evil spirit from God was upon Saul, that David took a harp, and played with his hand: so Saul was refreshed, and was well, and the evil spirit departed from him.
>
> —I Samuel 16:23, KJV

We see this spirit of fear, oppression, and unrest could come and go when another spirit breathed the presence of Adonai into the air. David had the ability to bring Saul out of torment and exhaustion and into a state of refreshment when he played the harp.

We gather more insight concerning spirits from Judges 9. Gideon, one of the great judges of Israel, had a son named Abimelech. He was the son of Gideon's concubine. Abimelech resorted to murdering seventy of his brothers, all but Jotham, the youngest son of Gideon. He ruled as a judge over Israel three years, but the Holy One took care of this man and his evil deeds using evil spirits:

> Abimelech ruled over Israel three years. And God sent an evil spirit between Abimelech and the leaders of Shechem,

and the leaders of Shechem dealt treacherously with Abimelech, that the violence done to the seventy sons of Jerubbaal might come, and their blood be laid on Abimelech their brother, who killed them, and on the men of Shechem, who strengthened his hands to kill his brothers.

–Judges 9:22-24, ESV

In I Chronicles 21, David takes a census of Israel and falls into sin and a plague breaks out and an angel with a sword is visible to King David:

Then God sent an angel to destroy Jerusalem, but as the angel was doing so, the LORD saw it and relented from the calamity, and He said to the angel who was destroying the people, "Enough! Withdraw your hand now!"

At that time the angel of the LORD was standing by the threshing floor of Ornanc the Jebusite.

When David lifted up his eyes and saw the angel of the LORD standing between heaven and earth, with a drawn sword in his hand stretched out over Jerusalem, David and the elders, clothed in sackcloth, fell facedown.

–I Chronicles 21: 15-16, BSB

The Father sent an angel to destroy King Herod:

> Now it happened that Herod was furious with the people of Tyre and Sidon. So they came to him, united. Having won over Blastus, the king's personal aide, they began asking for peace—because their country was supplied with food from the king's country.
>
> On an appointed day, Herod donned his royal robes and, taking his seat upon the throne, began to make a speech to them. The people were shouting, "The voice of a god and not a human!" Immediately, an angel of the Lord struck him down—because he did not give God the glory. And he was eaten by worms and died.
>
> –Acts 12:20-23 TLV

What a horrific death. But I must ask, how is it possible to cast out a spirit Adonai sent? The Body of Messiah must ponder such questions. What if the Father wants us to have a spirit? A spirit of humility is needed to be a leader. The Apostle Paul's testimony explains this best:

> And lest I should be exalted above measure through the abundance of the revelations, there was given to me a thorn in the flesh, the messenger of Satan to buffet me, lest I should be exalted above measure. For this thing I besought the Lord thrice, that it might depart from me.
>
> –II Corinthians 12:7-9, KJV

Paul tried three times to do self-deliverance, and nothing happened. This is the same Paul who was so anointed that his apron cloths healed people:

> And God wrought special miracles by the hands of Paul: So that from his body were brought unto the sick handkerchiefs or aprons, and the diseases departed from them, and the evil spirits went out of them.
>
> –Acts 19:11-12, KJV

The Father speaks to Paul about weakness and answers how suffering is one of the greatest tools for righteousness:

> And he said unto Paul, "My grace is sufficient for thee: for my strength is made perfect in weakness. Most gladly therefore will I rather glory in my infirmities, that the power of Christ may rest upon me."
>
> –II Corinthians 12:7-9, KJV

Some scholars believe Paul's weakness may have been his eyesight. He was blinded for three days and later healed. Many of his letters suggest this might have been his thorn. "See with what large letters I am writing to you with my own hand" (Galatians 6:11, NASB). Other writings suggest Paul indeed had a physical ailment:

> But you know that it was because of a bodily illness that I preached the gospel to you the first time; and that which

was a trial to you in my bodily condition you did not despise or loathe, but you received me as an angel of God, as Christ Jesus Himself. Where then is that sense of blessing you had? For I bear you witness that, if possible, you would have plucked out your eyes and given them to me.

–Galatians 4:13-15, NASB

When we study these passages concerning spirits, we learn that the Father is in control and often uses spirits to correct, rebuke, and destroy. Although this is not taught often in mainstream Christianity, the Bible mentions these circumstances repeatedly. In order to understand spirits, we must look at their origin and who controls them.

Chapter 7

SEMIKHAH, LAYING ON OF HANDS

A growing fear of spirits and demons transferring onto other believers and causing torment is prevalent among those in deliverance ministry and certain denominations. After a deliverance conference, I noticed multiple ministers complained of headaches, sleepiness, and ailments afflicting them after laying on hands (James 5:14) and praying for people who they believed to be tormented by demons. Unlike James 5, this doctrine of laying on of hands taken out of context comes from the Book of I Timothy: "Lay hands suddenly on no man, neither be partaker of other men's sins: keep thyself pure" (I Timothy 5:22, KJV). This passage written by Paul is not about people who are tormented or have demons or the transference of spirits but is regarding electing men and women for service. Paul was trying to teach Timothy how to care for the assembly in Ephesus. In I Timothy 5, Paul makes strong points about the office of eldership and how to take time and care before just laying hands on anyone:

> I charge thee before God, and the Lord Jesus Christ, and the elect angels, that thou observe these things without preferring one before another, doing nothing by partiality. Lay hands suddenly on no man, neither be partaker of other men's sins: keep thyself pure.
>
> —I Timothy 5:21-22, KJV

Paul instructed Timothy and the elders not to lay hands on a man they prefer more than another; do not show favoritism when electing an elder. Paul wanted Timothy to look at the person's character and their gifts before putting them into an office in the assembly, an office for which they were not qualified or knowledgeable and mature enough to take on:

> "Therefore, brothers, seek out from among you seven men who are known to be filled with the Set-apart Spirit and wisdom, whom we shall appoint for this duty, but we shall give ourselves continually to prayer and to serving the Word." And the word pleased the entire group. And they chose Stephanos, a man filled with belief and the Set-apart Spirit, and Philip, and Prochoros, and Nikanor, and Timon, and Parmenas, and Nikolaos, a convert from Antioch, whom they set before the emissaries. And when they had prayed, they laid hands on them.
>
> –Acts 6:3-6, ISR

The laying on of hands designates a person for a task:

> When you bring the Levites before the LORD, the people of Israel shall lay their hands on the Levites, and Aaron shall offer the Levites before the LORD as a wave offering from the people of Israel, that they may do the service of the LORD.
>
> –Leviticus 8:9-11, ESV

The Hebrew word *S'mikhah* or *Semikah* means authority and refers to the laying on of hands. It is given when a person places hands on the head of another. The laying on of hands is something that can be traced back to the time of Moses:

> So the LORD said to Moses, "Take Joshua the son of Nun, a man in whom is the Spirit, and lay your hand on him. Make him stand before Eleazar the priest and all the congregation, and you shall commission him in their sight. You shall invest him with some of your authority that all the congregation of the people of Israel may obey."
>
> –Numbers 27:18-20, ESV

In Numbers 11, Moses ordained seventy judges without laying any hands on them:

> So Moses went out and told the people the words of the LORD. And he gathered seventy men of the elders of the people and placed them around the tent. Then the LORD came down in the cloud and spoke to him, and took some of the Spirit that was on him {Moses} and put

it on the seventy elders. And as soon as the Spirit rested on them, they prophesied.

–Numbers 11:24-25, ESV

One popular belief taught today, termed "a transference of anointing" by the laying on of hands, is another doctrine that has crept in falsely. Bethel College in Redding, California, made the news in 2015 when some students laid on Smith Wigglesworth's grave to suck out his anointing. In the occult, they call it "grave sucking." The students wanted to receive Wigglesworth's anointing, which they referred to as supernatural, and thought they could soak up this power by lying on his grave. As if the anointing was something anyone could get just as quickly and easily as going through a fast-food drive-thru. What a sad condition to be in the same state as Simon, the sorcerer, who thought he could buy the anointing with money:

> Now when Simon saw that the *Ruach ha-Kodesh* was given through the laying on of hands by the emissaries, he offered them money, saying, "Give this power to me, too—so that anyone on whom I lay hands may receive the *Ruach ha-Kodesh*." Peter said to him, "May your silver go to ruin, and you with it—because you thought you could buy God's gift with money! You have no part or share in this matter, because your heart is not right before God. Therefore repent of this wickedness of yours, and pray to the Lord that, if possible, the intent of your heart

may be pardoned. For I see in you the poison of bitterness and the bondage of unrighteousness!"

–Acts 8:18-23, TLV

The person granting the *Semikah* (ordination) had to do so while accompanied by two or three others. The person ordained would be an expert in Jewish law (Torah) and qualified to rule in all areas. This anointing was exceptionally helpful, considering Moses dealt with the disputes of millions of Hebrews traveling on foot in the wilderness. Moses's father-in-law brings counsel to him and helps him delegate the people's needs to others:

> The next day, Moses sat to judge the people, and they stood around Moses from morning till evening. When Moses' father-in-law saw all that he did for the people, he said, "What's this you're doing to the people? Why sit by yourself, alone, with all the people standing around from morning until evening?"
>
> Moses answered his father-in-law, "It's because the people come to me to inquire of God. When they have an issue, it comes to me, and I judge between a man and his neighbor, so I make them understand God's statutes and His laws.

–Exodus 18:13-16, TLV

Moses' father-in-law suggested he appoint others under him to help with the less weighty matters. Later, the term "rabbi (teacher)" would come about, by which Yeshua was often referred. This title was passed down by the sages of the land of Israel who were ordained. As direct heirs to the Torah of Moses, they were granted authority to judge. The laying on of hands and the transference of spirits is a doctrine that has been incorporated into the text.

Yeshua states in Matthew 23, to not refer to any man as rabbi or teacher and to call no man on earth your father. "But you are not to be called rabbi; for One is your Teacher, and you are all brothers. And call no man on earth your father; for One is your Father, who is in heaven" (Matthew 23:8-9, TLV). This, too, has been misconstrued. Ephesians 4 lists apostles, prophets, teachers, and elders and says that Yeshua gave these roles until the Body of Messiah becomes unified and mature. In I John 2, we read about how we are to refer to mature leaders as fathers. So what was Yeshua saying in Matthew 23? He stated that they should not address these corrupt leaders as rabbis or fathers, as they did not keep His Father's commandments. Yeshua said these corrupt ones longed to receive accolades from men. Paul said, "For though you may have ten thousand guardians in Messiah, yet you do not have many fathers. For in Messiah *Yeshua*, I became your father through the Good News. I urge you therefore—be imitators of me" (I Corinthians 4:15-16, TLV).

The story from Acts 8, involving Simon, the sorcerer,

showcased how enamored Simon was and eager to buy the power the apostles had. The texts said that Simon practiced magic and amazed the people. The people looked upon this Simon as if he were a god. Philip came preaching the Good News, and Simon the sorcerer believed and was baptized, but later Simon becomes astonished by the miracles and healings that took place from the ministry of the apostles and attempted to purchase this with money. The text said, "Now when Simon saw that the *Ruach ha-Kodesh* was given through the laying on of hands by the emissaries, he offered them money." This man wanted power, but Peter knew he needed delivered:

> Peter said to him, "May your silver go to ruin, and you with it—because you thought you could buy God's gift with money! You have no part or share in this matter, because your heart is not right before God. Therefore, repent of this wickedness of yours, and pray to the Lord that, if possible, the intent of your heart may be pardoned.
>
> –Acts 8:18-22, TLV

Simon wanted to be in a place of the spotlight. He still wanted the people to look upon him as if he were a god. This laying on of hands was a gift, and one that Peter, Philip, and others had been given from the Holy One and Yeshua. Peter's anointing came from significant crushing, walking with Messiah, and being called and appointed. These men would have known the Torah and been deemed qualified to lead. They had no New Testament.

If Simon still had these demonic issues from his lifelong occupation of sorcery, wouldn't Peter have said, "Come out of him you spirit of witchcraft in the Name of Yeshua?"

On the contrary, we see Peter telling him it is a matter of the heart. Simon needs repentance. Most people who have been dabbling in the occult have many wounds and need counseling for complete healing. Sometimes in the deliverance ministry, many come wanting a touch leading to complete freedom, but the Father wants us to work out our salvation with fear and trembling. He wants us to learn and grow, becoming mature, humble, and producing much fruit. In I Timothy 5, where some acquire the scripture about laying hands on no man suddenly, it also talks about not bringing accusations against an elder but to bring two or three witnesses. This chapter has been misapplied.

According to Acts 19, Paul's handkerchiefs could deliver those with evil spirits:

> God was doing extraordinary miracles by Paul's hands, so that even handkerchiefs and aprons that touched his skin were brought to the sick, and the diseases left them and the evil spirits went out of them.
>
> —Acts 19:11-12, TLV

The Greek word for handkerchief *soudaria* is in Strong's Greek 4676: A handkerchief, napkin. Of Latin origin; a *sudarium*, i.e., Towel. These towels were used more than likely to wipe the sweat from their brow during the heat of the day. The word apron was a type of apron used to protect ones under clothing, but this could have also been an undergarment called the *tallit katan*. *Chaim Bentorah Biblical Hebrew Word Studies* has an insightful article explaining more on these mysterious aprons:

> The words used for handkerchiefs and aprons are really words which express the borders of his garments. The word for garment is *katan* is the Aramaic and is the exact word used today for the *tallit katan*. The *tallit katan* is a garment worn for possibly thousands of years by the Hebrews as a prayer shawl which had on its borders *tzitzits* or tassels. Most likely people snatched the tassels off Paul's *tallit katan* and used these for healing. [18]

These tassels or *tzitzitz (Tzitziyot* – plural) were exactly what the woman with the issue of blood touched:

> And there was a woman who had had a discharge of blood for twelve years, and though she had spent all her living on physicians, she could not be healed by anyone. She came up behind him and touched the fringe of his garment, and immediately her discharge of blood ceased. And Jesus said, "Who was it that touched me?"
>
> –Luke 8:43-45, ESV

---

[18] https://www.chaimbentorah.com/2014/06/word-study-healing-handkerchiefs/

Would this freedom from grasping hold of the *tzitziyot* be an extraordinary miracle if demons just jumped around and transferred to others nearby? What would that solve? At the time of Paul, exorcists had plenty of work because so many illnesses were attributed to evil spirits. Any complaint during that time, accompanied by disturbing behavior such as epilepsy, mental illness, or depression, was often explained in terms of demon possession.

In Acts 19, seven sons of Sceva attempted to do an exorcism but were met with an attack from the spirits. These Jewish exorcists were trying to use the name of Messiah Yeshua as a magic wand. One can learn much from their title. *Sceva* is *Strong's Hebrew* G4630 and means a left-handed mind reader. Since there was not a high priest in Jerusalem named Sceva, perhaps it was a translational error, and the priest was left-handed. These Sons of the man were, like Simon, the magician, psychic mind readers:

> But some traveling Jewish exorcists also tried to invoke the name of the Lord *Yeshua*, saying, "I charge you by the *Yeshua* whom Paul preaches." Seven sons of a Jewish ruling *kohen* named Sceva were doing this. But the evil spirit answered them, "I know *Yeshua* and I know about Paul, but who are you?"
>
> Then the man with the evil spirit sprang at them, subduing and overpowering all of them, so that they fled

out of that house naked and wounded.

–Acts 19:13-16, ESV

This news reached the people, both Jews and Greeks, and they began to fear Yeshua Messiah in Ephesus.

When we read of Jonah and the coming destruction of Nineveh, we see no deliverance ministry showing up: "Yet forty days, and Nineveh shall be overthrown" (Jonah 3:4, KJV). The city was so immoral that the Father was going to destroy it in forty days:

> And the people of Nineveh believed God. They called for a fast and put on sackcloth, from the greatest of them to the least of them. The word reached the king of Nineveh, and he arose from his throne, removed his robe, covered himself with sackcloth, and sat in ashes. And he issued a proclamation and published through Nineveh, "By the decree of the king and his nobles: Let neither man nor beast, herd nor flock, taste anything. Let them not feed or drink water, but let man and beast be covered with sackcloth, and let them call out mightily to God."

–Jonah 3:5-8, ESV

The people of Nineveh humbled themselves and fasted, and the Father spared them and the cattle. Fasting, repentance, and humility bring great deliverance.

Much of the New Testament has stories depicting demons, but there is not much concerning this topic in the *Tanakh* or Old Testament. What we can learn from this absence of Satan and demons in the Old Testament is something that happened in the Jewish world after the exile and with the influence of Hellenism. The term demon-possessed was often placed on the sick and suffering or those severely oppressed. Paradigm shifts in any society are created over time in slow increments. Our whole thinking process must be renewed. However, spiritual unrest and demonic strongholds will increase as the world grows darker and more people become encased in sin.

Spirits Unveiled: Book Two

Chapter 8

BINDING THE SPIRITS

Many times, the original meaning of certain passages of the Bible has been lost in translation, or the correct meaning is watered down over time. "Binding and Loosing" is a term used in many charismatic settings to expel demons, receive wealth, or release (loose) angels. The ministers usually prompt those suffering from sickness, addiction, poverty, or other areas of need to come down to the front of the congregation. The scene unfolds in this manner. The pastor or evangelist will begin to lay hands on the foreheads of each one standing before him and pray in this approach:

> *I bind you, you foul devil of lust! I bind every spirit of pornography. I bind every demon of torment and I loose ministering angels. I bind every spirit of addiction. I bind you Satan, and you cannot have these brothers and sisters in Jesus name!*

Although we do have power over demons, this is not what binding and loosing means.

The Torah (first five books of Moses) bestowed power to bind and loose in the Sanhedrin, the priesthood, and judges over Israel. The terms "bind and loose (forbid and permit)" appear thousands of times in the Mishnah and Talmud, an extensive collection of writings, containing a full account of the civil and religious laws of the Jews. *First Fruits of Zion*, a Messianic website that specializes in the study and teaching of Scripture from its historical, linguistic, and cultural context explains binding and loosing more plainly in their article *Binding and Loosing:*

> If one sage declared something as bound, he should not ask another sage who might declare it loosed. If two sages are both present and one rules something unclean and the other rules it clean, if one binds and the other looses, then if one of them is superior to the other in learning and number of disciples, follow his ruling. Otherwise, follow the stricter view. (b.Avodah Zarah 7a) [19]

The Rabbis of Yeshua's day added many man-made oral traditions to the Torah, making it a burden that was too heavy to bear at times. Yeshua's disciples/apostles were to be his successors. Yeshua vested his disciples and apostles with the same authority as that which he found belonging to the scribes and Pharisees. The unrighteous leadership had bound heavy

---

[19] https://torahportions.ffoz.org/disciples/matthew/the-power-to-bind-and-loose.html\

burdens on the people's shoulders but would not remove it, meaning "loose them of the weight."

In Numbers 30, Moses expresses to the people that if they make a vow with their mouths to the Lord or swear an oath, the person is to keep it. The oath or pledge was binding. Moses spoke to the heads of the tribes of the people of Israel, saying:

> This is what the LORD has commanded. If a man vows a vow to the LORD, or swears an oath to bind himself by a pledge, he shall not break his word. He shall do according to all that proceeds out of his mouth.
>
> –Numbers 30:1-2, ESV

Binding and loosing is never connected to deliverance from strongholds. When Yeshua or the apostles prayed over those suffering, there was no mention of binding and loosing. Yeshua often called the spirit or sickness by name:

1. " When *Yeshua* saw that a crowd was gathering fast, He rebuked the unclean spirit, telling it, "I command you, deaf and mute spirit, come out of him and do not ever enter him again!" (Mark 9:25, TLV).

2. " "Ah! What have we to do with You, *Yeshua* of *Natzeret*? Have You come to destroy us? I know who You are! You are the Holy One of God!" *Yeshua* rebuked him, saying, "Quiet! Come out of him!" And when the demon threw him down in their midst, it came out without hurting him. (Luke 4:35, TLV).

3. "And Jesus rebuked him, saying, 'Be quiet, and come out of him!'" (Mark 1:25, NASB).

Yeshua gave His apostles authority. Why would a minister want to bind a demon? Binding something keeps it here and keeps it attached to the person. Yeshua told the woman who was bound, "Woman thou art loosed" (Luke 13:12, KJV). Yeshua told the demons, "Go." He did not want them to be bound. He wanted the demons or sickness to flee.

Additionally, as a legal term, binding means to place under legal obligation by contract or oath. Deliverance ministers see binding and loosing as a form of binding the spirits and rendering them helpless. This formula is found nowhere in the Bible. The binding or loosing of the Torah should not be applied to demons. It was never written in that context. It was concerning the law/Torah and the ruling leaders. According to the *Jewish Encyclopedia*, this binding and declaring fast days could be strict:

> This does not mean that, as the learned men, they merely decided what, according to the Law, was forbidden or allowed, but that they possessed and exercised the power of tying or untying a thing by the spell of their divine authority, just as they could, by the power vested in them, pronounce and revoke an anathema upon a person. The various schools had the power "to bind and to loose"; that is, *to forbid and to permit*; and they could bind any day

by declaring it a fast-day. This power and authority, vested in the rabbinical body of each age or in the Sanhedrin, received its ratification and final sanction from the celestial court of justice (Sifra, Emor, ix.; Mak. 23b). [20]

In Matthew 16, Yeshua tells Peter He will give him keys to the kingdom and Peter will have the same authority, and this will involve mercy and freedom:

> And I will give unto thee the keys of the kingdom of heaven: and whatsoever thou shalt bind on earth shall be bound in heaven: and whatsoever thou shalt loose on earth shall be loosed in heaven.
>
> –Matthew 16:19, KJV

The Complete Jewish Bible translation reads more correctly:

> I will give you the keys of the Kingdom of Heaven. Whatever you prohibit on earth will be prohibited in heaven, and whatever you permit on earth will be permitted in heaven.
>
> –Matthew 16:19, CJB

Yeshua was giving spiritual keys of power and authority. After Yeshua mentions the keys, He informs Peter that whatever he permits on earth will be permitted in heaven, and whatever Peter

---

[20] BINDING AND LOOSING - JewishEncyclopedia.com

prohibits on earth will be prohibited in heaven. Binding and loosing are a rabbinical term. *The Jewish Encyclopedia* states:

> Binding and loosing (Hebrew: *asar ve-hittir*) . . . Rabbinical term for "forbidding and permitting." . . The power of binding and loosing was always claimed by the Pharisees. Under Queen Alexandra, the Pharisees say Josephus (Wars of the Jews 1:5:2), "became the administrators of all public affairs so as to be empowered to banish and readmit whom they pleased, as well as to loose and to bind. . ."
>
> *–The Jewish Encyclopedia*

"Binding and loosing" grants authority to make rulings within the framework of the Torah, either on how to employ the Torah in challenging situations or to establish traditions in areas in which the Torah is silent. These rulings are called *halacha* (Hebrew: "the Way") and concern our walk and keeping our Father's commandments. Messiah tells us that our righteousness must exceed the Pharisees and Sadducees:

> Do not think that I have come to abolish the Law or the Prophets; I have not come to abolish them but to fulfill them. For truly, I say to you, until heaven and earth pass away, not an iota, not a dot, will pass from the Law until all is accomplished. Therefore, whoever relaxes one of the least of these commandments and teaches others to do the

same will be called least in the kingdom of heaven, but whoever does them and teaches them will be called great in the kingdom of heaven. For I tell you, unless your righteousness exceeds that of the scribes and Pharisees, you will never enter the kingdom of heaven.

–Matthew 5:17-20, ESV

In Matthew 18, Yeshua mentions binding and loosing concerning a brother or sister who sins against another believer. Yeshua makes a point concerning two or three witnesses:

If your brother sins against you, go and tell him his fault, between you and him alone. If he listens to you, you have gained your brother. But if he does not listen, take one or two others along with you, that every charge may be established by the evidence of two or three witnesses. If he refuses to listen to them, tell it to the church. And if he refuses to listen even to the church, let him be to you as a Gentile and a tax collector. Truly, I say to you, whatever you bind on earth shall be bound in heaven, and whatever you loose on earth shall be loosed in heaven.

–Matthew 18:15-18, ESV

The Messiah is discussing a passage from the Torah, and He is giving counsel on how to go about addressing a situation with a fellow believer:

> You shall not hate your brother in your heart, but you shall reason frankly with your neighbor, lest you incur sin because of him.
>
> —Leviticus 19:3, ESV

Yeshua says if your brother or sister sins against you, you are to meet with them in private. If the person listens to you and admits their sins, you have won your brother back, but if he does not listen, you should take one or two others and confront him again. This completes the message on two or three being gathered. In Matthew 18, after Yeshua proclaims, "whatever we bind on earth shall be bound in heaven," He continues the message of forgiveness by repeating the two or three witnesses:

> Again I say to you, if two of you agree on earth about anything they ask, it will be done for them by my Father in heaven. For where two or three are gathered in my name, there am I among them.
>
> —Matthew 18:19-20, ESV

Throughout the Bible, we are told that every matter is established by two or three witnesses:

> This is the third time I am coming to you. "Every matter must be established by the testimony of two or three witnesses."
>
> —II Corinthians 13:1, BSB

The formula for binding and loosing concerning brothers or sisters who sin against a person is binding and requires the following steps. If the person in sin repents, the other party must forgive him. But what if he does not repent? The person is told to bring it to the attention of the leaders/elders of the community. Now the sin would no longer be a private issue, and if the person still refuses to repent, Yeshua says to treat them like a pagan or a tax collector. Yeshua ate with sinners and tax collectors. He said the sick need a doctor. These instructions were for those who were in covenant, had been born anew, and were part of the community. But then, moving past this part of the story, we discover a scripture that Saints use all over the world to receive what they want from God. It is called "The Agreement Prayer." How many times have we repeated this prayer with two or three touching anything -- and nothing happened? This is not to take away from the power of prayer or praying together. The Father said, "If you abide in me and my words abide in you, ask me whatsoever you will and I will do it" (John 15:7, KJV). He also said, "How can two walk together if they are not in agreement?" (Amos 3:3, KJV). So yes, if two or three agree and have a relationship with Him, the request may be answered, but to go deeper:

> Truly, I say to you, whatever you bind on earth shall be bound in heaven, and whatever you loose on earth shall be loosed in heaven. Again I say to you, if two of you agree on earth about anything they ask, it will be done for them

by my Father in heaven. For where two or three are gathered in my name, there am I among them. Then Peter came up and said to him, "Lord, how often will my brother sin against me, and I forgive him? As many as seven times?"

–Matthew 18:18-21, ESV

Peter's response seems out of place unless we understand what the topic is about. Yeshua answers: "I do not say to you seven times, but seventy-seven times" (Matthew 18:22, ESV). Two or more made it a binding contract, and the person who would not repent was asked to separate himself from the Body of Yeshua and repent:

> For if we go on sinning deliberately after receiving the knowledge of the truth, there no longer remains a sacrifice for sins, but a fearful expectation of judgment, and a fury of fire that will consume the adversaries. Anyone who has set aside the law of Moses dies without mercy on the evidence of two or three witnesses. How much worse punishment, do you think, will be deserved by the one who has trampled underfoot the Son of God, and has profaned the blood of the covenant by which he was sanctified, and has outraged the Spirit of grace?
>
> –Hebrews 10:26-29, ESV

Also, John 8:17 says, "It is also written in your law, {Torah} that the testimony of two men is true" (KJV). If a person were accused of breaking the commandments or sinning, the matter had to go before those in authority, and there had to be two or three witnesses to bring accusations. This is a binding Torah commandment. Again, binding and loosing has nothing to do with expelling demons. As a legal term, binding means to place under legal obligation by contract or oath.

Chapter 9

UNFORGIVENESS AND DEMONS

Torment is something that cripples a person and leads to panic attacks and anxiousness. King Saul was a man in torment. His affliction must have been horrific, for even King Saul's servants confronted him:

> And Saul's servants said to him, "Behold now, a harmful spirit from God is tormenting you. Let our lord now command your servants who are before you to seek out a man who is skillful in playing the lyre, and when the harmful spirit from God is upon you, he will play it, and you will be well."
>
> –I Samuel 16:15-16, ESV

There seemed to be only one cure to make the demons flee: sweet music. The Israeli harp was called a *Nevel*, and each string, when plucked, would have spelled out the ancient Jewish script of our Father's Word. As David (Future King of Israel) plucked each string, he may have spelled out a message of deliverance. The oppression left immediately. There was just one problem: the dark spirits came back.

Tormenting spirits were not just a problem King Saul had, there are still those suffering from this torment today. Once while my husband and I were trying to bring healing to a tortured soul, I kept hearing in my spirit that there was grave unforgiveness. The home I stood in needed freedom. I asked the woman, thin, frail, and consumed with cancer, who the large dark man towering over her was that I kept seeing in the spirit. She began to tell me about her ex-husband and the horrific abuse she had suffered at his hands. I then shared a story about a young man sodomized by his father's drunken friends one night. This man went on to become a minister and went to prisons spreading the gospel of Yeshua. One night after teaching on forgiveness, grace, and salvation, he made an altar call at a prison. A prisoner came down front and began to repent, weeping. After the service, the prisoner approached the pastor and thanked him for his forgiveness and the message of hope. The minister soon realized he was face to face with one of the men who had sodomized him in his youth. In that instant, he knew he had not forgiven the man. Hatred sprang forth in his heart.

After sharing the story, the pale lady lying in bed began to look at me with astonishment, and she said, "I know why you are telling me that story. My son was brutally assaulted and sodomized repeatedly. Several men kept him locked in a basement for days. My son was never the same. I cannot forgive them! I don't believe God is going to send me to hell to burn in flames because of my unforgiveness, do you?" I felt tiny in that moment sitting on her bed. I had no words at the tip of my tongue to speak. I remember taking her hand, and my husband and I prayed with her. I said, "Abba Father, help her to want to forgive these men." I told her I could not understand such grief. I had no way to measure such torment, but I managed to explain that I believed this unforgiveness had caused much of the sickness in her physical body, and she agreed. I told her that she was not hurting the men by not forgiving them, she was hurting herself. Before we left, I was able to hold her. I held her with all the love I could muster for such frailty, and, finally, the tears began to flow from her eyes. I knew then that forgiveness had begun. Later, we learned that she was becoming whole, and cancer had left.

Unforgiveness is one of the most significant obstacles and entryways for torment and oppression. In Matthew 18, there is a parable in the Bible about an unforgiving servant. The story is about a king and one of his servants who owed him a large sum. The king commanded him to be sold, along with his wife, children, and all that he had, for payment. The servant fell on his knees and cried out for mercy, and the great king had compassion and forgave him of all his debt. But then the story takes a turn one would not expect. The forgiven man found a fellow servant who owed him a small amount, only a tiny fraction of what he owed the king. He grabbed him, and he screamed at him, "Pay me what you owe me!" He then found the man had no money, so he had him thrown in prison. Even though the now imprisoned man begged for patience, it seemed the forgiven man had forgotten the vast debt paid for him:

> When his fellow servants saw what had taken place, they were greatly distressed, and they went and reported to their master all that had taken place. Then his master summoned him and said to him, "You wicked servant! I forgave you all that debt because you pleaded with me. And should not you have had mercy on your fellow servant, as I had mercy on you?" And in anger his master delivered him to the jailers, until he should pay all his debt. So also my heavenly Father will do to every one of you, if you do not forgive your brother from your heart.
>
> —Matthew 18:31-35, ESV

The great King had mercy and forgave the servant, but the servant could not forgive others. Yeshua suffered so greatly that He was unrecognizable. He was beaten to such a bloody mess that it was difficult to tell that He was even human, and yet He said, "Father, forgive them, for they know not what they do" (Luke 23: 34, ESV). Notice in the parable, the man who could not forgive was delivered to the tormentors. The word torment means to inflict with anguish and severe agony. Torment came upon King Saul because he had a root of bitterness and a problem with disobedience. Saul was fearful of David taking the kingship from him, and a murderous spirit sprang up in his heart due to jealousy. "And Saul was furious and resented this song. "They have ascribed tens of thousands to David," he said, "but only thousands to me. What more can he have but the kingdom?" And from that day forward, Saul kept a jealous eye on David" (I Samuel 18:8-9, TLV). Adonai sent demons to torment Saul, and the very man he wants to hunt down like a flea, is the young man, David, who brings relief from his torment:

> Saul said to his courtiers, "Find me someone who can play well and bring him to me."
>
> One of the young men answered and said, "I have seen a son of Jesse the Beth-lehemite who is skillful in playing music. He is a mighty man of valor, a warrior, prudent in speech, a handsome man, and *Adonai* is with him."
>
> –I Samuel 16:17-18, TLV

Remember, unforgiveness hurts the one holding onto it, not the person who inflicted it. How many times have we hurt the one who died for us? Too many times to count:

> And if children, also heirs—heirs of God and joint-heirs with Messiah—if indeed we suffer with Him so that we may also be glorified with Him.
>
> –Romans 8:17, TLV

> For if you forgive others their trespasses, your heavenly Father will also forgive you, but if you do not forgive others their trespasses, neither will your Father forgive your trespasses.
>
> —Matthew 6:14-15, ESV

We will have many sorrows in this world, but thanks to Yeshua, He has overcome the world. Sometimes we invite the tormenting spirits by not being obedient, having envy, or wrongful actions toward others. At other times we are hated by the world because we stand for righteousness. In Matthew 10, Yeshua warns that we will be hated: "And you will be hated by all because of My name, but the one who endures to the end shall be saved" (Matthew 10:22, TLV). Forgiveness, at times, can be complicated depending on the offense. When being stoned to death, Stephen spoke the exact words as the Messiah: "forgive them for they know not what they do." The woman physically sick with cancer had to forgive those who abused her son to begin the healing process.

Rick Nauert, PhD, author of *Bitterness Can Make You Sick* discusses the effects of bitterness and unforgiveness on the body, physical and mental health. Psychologist Dr. Carsten Wrosch has spent fifteen years researching the topic and has recently focused his attention on the impact of bitterness:

Persistent bitterness may result in global feelings of anger and hostility that, when strong enough, could affect a person's physical health," said psychologist Dr. Carsten Wrosch. "When harbored for a long time," Wrosch said, "bitterness may forecast patterns of biological dysregulation (a physiological impairment that can affect metabolism, immune response or organ function) and physical disease." [21]

To remove the torment from our lives, we need to make sure we are not harboring bitterness, unforgiveness, anger, jealousy, or fear lest we end up like King Saul or the man mentioned in the parable by Yeshua in Matthew 18. The man who was forgiven much was unable to forgive a small debt. He was filled with rage and turned over to the tormentors. One translation says the jailer. Sadly, we often entomb ourselves in our own prisons.

---

[21] Bitterness Can Make You Sick (psychcentral.com)

Chapter 10

SICKNESS AND DISEASE

Years ago, when I was severely sick with a neurological disease and fibromyalgia, I attended a small assembly with a kind pastor. I noticed the pastor often looked at me with a peculiar expression. His eyes would shift to my cane and my wobbly legs, then gaze back up as if he were analyzing why I needed an instrument for balance at such a tender age. On one occasion, he prayed for me with a loud, boisterous voice. "Father, get to the root of this sickness, the very root!" I felt as if the root he may have been referring to was possibly unconfessed sins. The pastor had suggested more than once that sickness can be a spiritual issue. I wondered if he thought the origin was something unholy in my life, like pride, lust, or anger. I remembered the scripture in Timothy about laying hands on the sick and seeing them recover. It also said, "And if they have sinned it shall be forgiven them" (James 5:13-15, KJV).

Many well-known evangelists and pastors had prayed over

me, but I was still suffering horribly. I pondered this and went over a list of people I had forgiven and the prayers I had prayed for the Father to search me and cleanse me. I cried out to the Holy One that I knew I had sinned and had things I needed to work on, like most of us do, but I still felt awkward in the presence of this pastor. It seemed every time he prayed for me it was suggested I might be responsible for this disease. I felt like Job's friends surrounded me at my assembly. Of course, I was no Job; my past had its colorful moments. But I had returned to the Father with all my heart.

The following Thursday night Bible study was quite a shock for me. I waddled in on my cane, and there was the pastor with one shoe off. His right foot looked swollen, and he was using a cane. Gout had set in his foot. Had the Holy One allowed this to happen for a reason? I wasn't sure, but I felt quite relieved that a minister I deemed righteous could also go through pain. It was confirmation that perhaps it happens to the best of us. He spoke about how his gout had caused him to be still before the Lord because he couldn't go to work and how he had a wonderful time in prayer at home resting. Sickness can be an unusual friend at times.

Have you ever wondered who the first person to become sick was in the Bible? Job would be the first, and the next person written about was Jacob. After Jacob wrestled with an angel all night, his hip was out of the socket, and he walked with a limp afterward. Indeed, he walked with a limp until the day his sons buried him. Hosea says this about Jacob, "Yea, he had power over the angel and prevailed" (Hosea 12:4, KJV). The devil had nothing to do with maiming Jacob; it was an angel. We have been taught that angels only protect us; this one wrestled with Jacob and injured him.

Sickness and disease are mentioned in full detail in the Torah. In Deuteronomy 28, there is a short list of blessings due to obedience and a rather lengthy list of curses due to disobedience. These curses would fall upon the nations and Adonai's people if they turned to idolatry and did not keep Adonai's commandments and statutes:

> The Lord will send upon you curses, confusion, and rebuke, in all you undertake to do, until you are destroyed and until you perish quickly, on account of the evil of your deeds, because you have forsaken me. The Lord will make the pestilence cling to you until He has consumed you from the land where you are entering to possess it. The Lord will smite you with consumption and with fever and with inflammation and with fiery heat and with the sword and with blight and with mildew, and they will pursue you until you perish. The heaven which is over your head shall be bronze, and the earth which is under you, iron. The Lord will make the rain of your land powder and dust; from heaven it shall come down on you until you are

destroyed. The Lord will smite thee with the botch of Egypt and with tumors, scabs and itch, sickness that cannot be healed.

–Deuteronomy 28:20-24, 27, ESV

Every sickness and plague, including all the diseases of Egypt, are promised to be sent by the Holy One on His people who fall into idolatry.

Many times, the children of Israel were sick or even died due to complaining and bitterness in the wilderness. Snakes sent from Adonai bit them, and the quail they requested came up through their nostrils. The earth even swallowed some:

> The LORD sent fiery serpents among the people, and they bit the people; and much people of Israel died.

–Numbers 21:6, KJV

Miriam spoke against Moses, and the Lord struck her with leprosy. Afterward, Moses begged Adonai to restore her, and He did. Yes, repeatedly, sickness was caused by sin. However, we know this is not always the case. For instance, look at Job and all his troubles.

Calvinism teaches that man is born totally depraved and separated from God. In Hebrew thought we are born sinless, but all are imperfect, being inclined to fall into sin. Many different denominations in Christianity suggests when Adam and Eve fell, sickness came into existence, and Adam and Eve (*Chavvah*) were cursed. The Word says something different:

> Cursed is the ground for thy sake; in sorrow shalt thou eat of it all the days of thy life; thorns and thistles shall it bring forth.
>
> –Genesis 3:17-18, KJV

This curse on the soil is followed by Adam's son Cain after he killed his brother:

> And the LORD said, "What have you done? The voice of your brother's blood is crying to me from the ground. And now you are cursed from the ground, which has opened its mouth to receive your brother's blood from your hand. When you work the ground, it shall no longer yield to you its strength."
>
> –Genesis 4:10-12, ESV

After the flood, Noah came out of the ark and built an altar to the Holy One and the curse on the ground and upon the earth was broken:

> Then Noah built an altar to the LORD and took some of every clean animal and some of every clean bird and offered burnt offerings on the altar. And when the LORD smelled the pleasing aroma, the LORD said in his heart, I will never again curse the ground because of man, for the

intention of man's heart is evil from his youth. Neither will I ever again strike down every living creature as I have done. While the earth remains, seedtime and harvest, cold and heat, summer and winter, day and night, shall not cease.

–Genesis 8:20-22, ESV

Although Adam was disobedient and ate from the tree of knowledge, of good and evil, Adam lived to be nine hundred and thirty years old. That is a ripe old age. Moses lived to be a hundred and twenty years old. We are told Moses's eyes were not dim, and his natural force was undiminished. Moses still had the strength of a young man. There was no sickness in his death. Sickness wasn't something we hear Adam or Eve dying from. Nor was it something Abraham or Isaac had, but Elisha, one of the mightiest prophets, died of a disease. "Now Elisha was fallen sick of his sickness whereof he died" (II Kings 13:14, KJV). Elisha raised the dead, made an ax head float, and caused Naaman to dip seven times, which cured him of leprosy, yet he died of his sickness. Years later, a dead man was thrown into Elisha's tomb, landed on his bones, and was revived. The dead man came back to life and stood upon his feet. Elisha may have died of sickness and disease, but Adonai's Word was still shut up in his bones, and his bones brought life:

> So Elisha died, and they buried him. Now bands of Moabites used to invade the land in the spring of the year.

And as a man was being buried, behold, a marauding band was seen and the man was thrown into the grave of Elisha, and as soon as the man touched the bones of Elisha, he revived and stood on his feet.

–II Kings 13:20-21, ESV

Sickness and death are not something that happened only during the days preceding Messiah Yeshua. It happened after Yeshua's ascension. Several missionaries who were with Paul became sick, and Paul could not heal them. He told the people that these men had risked their lives for the sake of the gospel, Epaphroditus, and a man named Trophimus: "Erastus abode at Corinth; but Trophimus have I left at Miletum sick" (II Timothy 4:20, KJV). Both men were doing work for the Father, and both men were with Paul. Paul was the apostle who could heal the sick with his apron (*tallit katan*/prayer shawl). Why would Paul leave a man sick if he could heal him? Why then were they not healed?

Sickness can be challenging to grasp. Paul told Timothy, "Be no longer a drinker of water, but use a little wine for thy stomach's sake and thine often infirmities" (I Timothy 5:23, KJV). The water in ancient times was not always fit to drink, and the wine helped kill parasites and bacteria. Paul doesn't say, "Timothy, don't speak your stomach troubles, don't even claim them. Life and death are in the power of the tongue. Tell the devil where to go!" No, that does not happen. When meditating on sickness and disease, we must consider the earth is getting old.

We have polluted it badly with factories, chemicals, landfills, oil spills, and water no longer fit to drink in many areas. New concern over the years has caused many people to start homesteading. They are raising their own food and caring for poultry and livestock. Not only are people starting to garden, but they are also growing herbs and using oils as medicine.

In II Kings 20, a king named Hezekiah will be given a cake of figs as medicine. Hezekiah is given a death sentence by the Holy One. The prophet Isaiah is told to visit this king and tell him to get his house in order because the Lord is going to take his life:

> In those days Hezekiah became mortally ill. So Isaiah the prophet son of Amoz came to him and said to him, "Thus says *Adonai*: Put your house in order. For you are dying, and will not live."
>
> –II Kings 20:1, TLV

Can you imagine being greeted with this type of Word from the Father? Hezekiah was around forty years old. Hezekiah began to weep before Adonai. He reminded the Holy One how he had served Him with a perfect heart. Before Isaiah the prophet left, the Holy One told him to go back and speak to Hezekiah:

> Return, and say to Hezekiah the leader of My people, thus says *Adonai*, the God of your father David: "I have heard your prayer and I have seen your tears. Behold, I am going to heal you. On the third day you will go up to the House

of *Adonai*. Then I will add 15 years to your life. I will deliver you and this city from the hand of the king of Assyria; I will defend this city for My own sake, and for My servant David's sake."

Then Isaiah said, "Take a cake of figs." So they took one and laid it on the boil, and he recovered.

–II Kings 20:5-7, ESV

Yes, weeping and crying out to the Holy One can bring restoration, but notice good reliable figs are brought to lay on the boil. Hezekiah gained fifteen years of his life.

When studying sickness and healing in the Bible, the process in which countless miracles occur is quite fascinating. In II Kings 4, Elijah laid his body upon the Shunammite's son who had died, and then the boy sneezed seven times and came back to life. In II Kings 5, Naaman had to dip seven times in water far from clean to receive his healing. Blind Barnabas cried out to Yeshua for his healing. The people tried to quiet him, but he would not give in. One blind man was healed after Yeshua took some clay or mud, spat on it, and placed it on his eyeball. Then the man was instructed to wash his eyes in a pool of water.

In Matthew 15, a woman's daughter is vexed with a demon. Yeshua never met her daughter in person, but the demon left her. In several of the Gospels, Yeshua told the person healed that their sins had been forgiven, but what exactly did he mean by this statement? In Matthew 9, Yeshua got into a boat and came to his hometown. "Then behold, they brought to Him a paralytic lying on a bed. When Jesus saw their faith, He said to the paralytic, "Son, be of good cheer; your sins are forgiven you." (Matthew 9:2, NKJ). This passage has been translated in error. Dr. Skip Moen unravels this peculiar passage at *Hebrew Word Study* blog in his article *Rooftop Faith:*

> Now the Greek, the Aramaic and the Delitzsch Hebrew gospels all have the phrase "Take heart" as an imperative. Another English version says, "Be comforted, my son" (although the Greek apparently omits the possessive pronoun and says simply, "son"). Howard's Hebrew text, however, says something quite different. The phrase translated from Greek as "take heart" is not imperative – it is reflexive; the word *titchazzek* literally means "You have strengthened yourself. [22]

The passage in its original context would have read, "And Yeshua saw their faith and he said, 'You have strengthened yourself, my son; by the faithfulness of God, your iniquities are taken from you.'" This sounds very different than, 'Take heart, my son; your sins are forgiven."

Yeshua felt virtue go out of Him when He healed the woman with the issue of blood (Luke 8:43-48). Other times, Yeshua did

---
[22] Rooftop Faith – Hebrew Word Study | Skip Moen

not heal them; he waited until they were dead like Martha's brother, Lazarus (John 11:43). Martha lacked faith, but it did not stop her brother from coming forth from the tomb. Stubborn sickness that stays is often blamed on lack of faith, wrong confessions, and hidden sin or Satan. How can a miracle or healing occur without sickness and suffering?

> As he passed by, he saw a man blind from birth. And his disciples asked him, "Rabbi, who sinned, this man or his parents, that he was born blind?" Jesus answered, "It was not that this man sinned, or his parents, but that the works of God might be displayed in him."
>
> –John 9:1-3, ESV

Moses told Adonai that he was not eloquent or good at making speeches, but Adonai answered him curiously: "Who has made man's mouth? Or who makes the dumb or deaf, or the seeing, or the blind? Have not I the Father?" (Exodus 4:11, KJV). Some in leadership would call blindness, deafness, and paralysis a curse from Satan. Multiple formulas for how to be cured have come about over time. Some of these instructions are harmful to sheep. Numerous Bible stories show that after significant sickness and years of suffering, the person's healing caused many to turn to the Father, like Aeneas:

> Peter went here and there among them all. He came down as well to the *kedoshim* living in Lydda. There he found a

man named Aeneas, who had been bedridden for eight years—he was paralyzed. Peter said to him, "Aeneas, Messiah *Yeshua* heals you. Get up and pack up your bed." Immediately, he got up! All who lived in Lydda and the Plain of Sharon saw him, and they turned to the Lord.

–Acts 9:32-35, TLV

Peter did not ask the Father to get to the root of Aeneas's sickness. He did not plead the blood over Aeneas or break generational curses. Peter did not bind anything. Peter did not say, "Aeneas, I'm sorry, but you just don't have enough faith right now. Study the chapter on faith in Hebrews 11 for a few more years, and I will be back to lay hands on you." The Body of Messiah must stop inflicting this sort of shame and guilt on those who are suffering. I have seen countless people go off their medication and become severely sick, especially the mentally ill. One person instructed to go off her medications ended up killing her pets and was placed in a facility. Of course, one touch from the Holy One can heal anyone, but this does not always come, not even to those servants as humble as Job.

King David gives wisdom and describes how suffering changes us on the inside:

> Before I was afflicted I went astray, but now I keep Your word.

–Psalm 119: 67, TLV

David continues in verse 71:

> It is good for me that I have been afflicted; that I might learn thy statutes. I know, O Lord, that thy judgments are right, and that thou in faithfulness hast afflicted me.

A Psalm of Asaph showcases the wealthy and healthy to a frightening degree:

> For I was envious of the arrogant when I saw the prosperity of the wicked. For they have no pangs until death; their bodies are fat and sleek. They are not in trouble as others are; they are not stricken like the rest of humankind. Therefore pride is their necklace; violence covers them as a garment. Their eyes swell out through fatness; their hearts overflow with follies. They scoff and speak with malice; loftily they threaten oppression. They set their mouths against the heavens, and their tongue struts through the earth.
>
> –Psalm 73:3-9, ESV

Job makes a comment to his wife after she tells him to curse the Holy One and die due to his sickness and great loss. He tells her she speaks as a foolish woman would speak. "What? Shall we receive good at the hand of God and not receive evil?" (Job 2:10, KJV). In Luke 14, a parable told by Messiah Yeshua highlights healthy people and sick, blind, lame people. Surprisingly it was the healthy and wealthy who had no time for the King of Kings:

But *Yeshua* said to him, "A certain man was hosting a large banquet, and he invited many. At the time for the banquet, he sent his slave to tell those who had been invited, 'Come, everything is already prepared.'

"But every one of them began to beg off. The first said to him, 'I bought a farm, and I'm obligated to go out to see it. I'm asking you to have me excused.' Then another one said, 'I've purchased five teams of oxen, and I'm going to check them out. I'm asking you to have me excused.' Still another said, 'I've married a wife, so I cannot come.'

"The slave came and reported these things to his master. Then the master of the house got angry and said to his slave, 'Quickly go out into the squares and alleys of the city and bring here the poor, the maimed, the blind, and the lame.'

"And the slave said, 'Master, I have done as you instructed, and still there is room.'

"So the master said to the slave, 'Go out into the thoroughfares and fenced areas, and press them to come in so my home may be filled. For I tell you, none of those men who were invited will taste my banquet.'"

–Luke 14:16-24, TLV

The wealthy, busy people of the world rejected his invitation, but not the sick and the poor. Why were they so willing to come?

Sickness and poverty can humble a person significantly and cause them to realize that they need a Savior in more ways than one. Spiritually blind people long to see.

The apostle Paul (Greek name) or Saul (Sha'ul), Hebrew, had a spiritual awakening after being struck with blindness for three days. Paul started as one of the primary persecutors of the followers of Yeshua. One day Paul was on his way to Damascus he saw a bright light shining down from heaven, and he heard a voice, and he fell on the ground:

Who are You, Lord?" Saul said.

"I am *Yeshua*—whom you are persecuting. But get up and go into the city, and you will be told what you must do."

The men travelling with him stood speechless, hearing the voice but seeing no one. Saul got up from the ground—but opening his eyes, he could see nothing. They led him by the hand and brought him into Damascus. For three days he could not see, and he did not eat or drink.

–Acts 9:6-9, TLV

The Holy One got Paul's attention by striking him with blindness. He humbled Paul. Paul fasted and prayed during those three days. The Father proclaims that He will show Paul how greatly he must suffer for His name's sake. And boy did he. Paul was stoned to death and saw the third heaven-- imprisoned, beaten, and shipwrecked at sea. Paul wrote at least seven books in the

New Testament. Through his suffering, he became a humble apostle. He also said he was given a thorn in his flesh, a messenger from Satan to buffet him. He asked the Lord three times to take it away:

> So that I would not exalt myself, a thorn in the flesh was given to me—a a messenger of satan to torment me, so I would not exalt myself. I pleaded with the Lord three times about this, that it might leave me. But He said to me, "My grace is sufficient for you, for power is made perfect in weakness." Therefore I will boast all the more gladly in my weaknesses, so that the power of Messiah may dwell in me. For Messiah's sake, then, I delight in weaknesses, in insults, in distresses, in persecutions, in calamities. For when I am weak, then I am strong.
>
> –II Corinthians 12:7-10, TLV

Some believe the thorn Paul was given was bad eyesight—blindness. He must write with large handwriting due to his vision: "Notice the large letters—I am writing to you with my own hand" (Galatians 6:11, TLV). Our bodies are supposed to get old. Paul said we are wasting away, yet inwardly we are being renewed day by day. I hear people say, "Yeshua healed all." However, Yeshua clearly did not heal every infirmity. Yeshua had trouble in His hometown:

> "A prophet is not without honor except in his own country, among his own relatives, and in his own house." He could do no mighty work there, except that He laid His hands on a few sick people and healed them. And He marveled because of their unbelief.
>
> –Mark 6:4-6, KJV

There was unbelief in Mark 6, this resulted in a lack of healing. In John 5, one man at the pool of Bethesda was healed, but we don't read anywhere in that story that the many others lying there were healed also. There is the story, long after Yeshua's resurrection and ascension, about a man who was laid at the Temple gate for years:

> And a man lame from birth was being carried, whom they laid daily at the gate of the temple that is called the Beautiful Gate to ask alms of those entering the temple. Now a man who was lame from birth was being carried to the Temple gate called Beautiful, where he was put every day to beg from those going into the Temple courts.
>
> –Acts 3:2, ESV

Now we know Yeshua walked into the Temple often, on every Sabbath, and at the hour of prayer. Yeshua must have passed this man who was laid at the gate of the Temple daily. Long after Yeshua's ascension, the man was made whole after Peter and John prayed for him.

The Bible contains many layers concerning sickness and disease, blessings, and curses. And some of the most righteous people in the Bible suffered more than anyone else. How can we forget righteous Job or the mighty prophet Elisha who died of his disease? The New Testament (B'rit Hadasha) deals with sickness as well. Missionaries with Paul are sent home carefully.

One day when the Messiah returns, the many questions concerning the topic of sickness, suffering, and pain will be answered. In the meantime, may we be compassionate to the sick and those suffering, remembering that when the disciples asked Yeshua who had sinned, the blind man or his parents, that he was born blind, the Master said neither this man nor his parents sinned. He was born blind so that the Holy One may be revealed. The Holy One always opens the eyes of the spiritually blind when they humbly ask. Following Yeshua's brother's instructions, the Body of Messiah must lay hands on the sick, anoint them with oil, and pray that they recover:

> Is any sick among you? let him call for the elders of the church; and let them pray over him, anointing him with oil in the name of the Lord: And the prayer of faith shall save the sick, and the Lord shall raise him up; and if he have committed sins, they shall be forgiven him.
>
> –James 5:14-15, KJV

James expresses that sin is a sickness, and the Holy One is a loving Father whose mercies are made new each morning.

Spirits Unveiled: Book Two

Chapter 11

MENTAL ILLNESS

The list of mental illnesses acknowledged by the Department of Psychiatry is lengthy. Some of the classifications that fall under mental conditions are quite surprising: Alcohol abuse, depression, ADHD, dyslexia, and sleep disorders appear on the list next to schizophrenia and bipolar disorder. The word mental involves the mind and insanity. Nearly one in five U.S. adults live with a mental illness (51.5 million in 2022). Mental illness includes many different conditions that vary in degree of severity, ranging from mild to moderate to severe. [23]

Certain denominations and non-denominational churches believe mental illness comes from Satan, sin, or both. When confronted by the spiritual leaders in Yeshua's day, Yeshua and John were accused of being demon-possessed:

> The Jews answered him, "Are we not right in saying that you are a Samaritan and have a demon?" Jesus answered,

---
[23] About Mental Health (cdc.gov)

"I do not have a demon, but I honor my Father, and you dishonor me."

–John 8:48-49, ESV

The Jews said to him, "Now we know that you have a demon! Abraham died, as did the prophets, yet you say, 'If anyone keeps my word, he will never taste death.'"

–John 8:52, ESV

For John came neither eating nor drinking, and they say, "He has a demon."

–Matthew 11:18, ESV

And the scribes who came down from Jerusalem were saying, "He is possessed by Beelzebub," and "by the prince of demons he casts out the demons."

–Mark 3:22, ESV

In the passages above, the ones bringing accusations of demonic issues were the ones who were spiritually sick.

Good health requires spiritual, physical, and mental well-being. Our God is a God of order. The Holy One gave careful instructions in His Word on how to take care of our bodies and the earth. Obedience in keeping the Lord's commandments and instructions for a blessed life brings order. When Adonai created the earth and placed Adam and Eve (*Chavah*), in the garden it was good. "And God saw everything that he had made, and, behold, it was very good" (Genesis 1:31, KJV). The Holy One cares for all of His creation. The word ("good") is *"tov"* in Hebrew, and it means to be functioning in divine order. Jeff Benner, author, and teacher specializing in the Ancient Hebrew alphabet, language, and culture, defines good and evil Hebraically:

> The first use of this word (*tov*) is in Genesis chapter one where *Elohiym* (Mighty One) calls his handiwork "good" (as it is usually translated). It should always be remembered that the Hebrew's often relate descriptions to functionality. When Elohiym looked at his handiwork, He did not see that it was "good," He saw that it was "functional" --like a well-oiled and tuned machine. In contrast to this word is the Hebrew word "*ra."* These two words, *tov* and *ra,* are used for the tree of the knowledge of "good" and "evil." While "*ra"* is often translated as evil it is best translated as "dysfunctional." [24]
>
> –Jeff Benner--Hebrew Research Center

The Holy One designed the earth to function in a divine order of operation. The food chain, the solar system, and the whole work of Adonai's Hands created a perfect model that flowed. This is good and functional. But man has polluted the

---

[24] https://www.ancient-hebrew.org/definition/good.htm

beautiful earth the Holy One created with oil spills, garbage, toxic waste, pharmaceutical drugs, and genetically modified seeds that will not reproduce. Toxic cancer-causing foods are sprayed with pesticides. Chickens are pumped with hormones, and livestock are fed genetically modified corn unconsumable for humans. Many animals are caged without sunlight or fresh air or are confined in tiny compartments. Many cattle are force fed as they stand in their own waste. Lagoons filled with pig waste leak, and the untreated waste enters rivers and other water bodies, killing the fish. One article titled *Lagoons of Pig waste are Overflowing* highlights the severity of the situation:

> When a pig in a large-scale farm urinates or defecates, the waste falls through slatted floors into holding troughs below. Those troughs are periodically flushed into an earthen hole in the ground called a lagoon in a mixture of water, pig excrement, and anaerobic bacteria. The bacteria digest the slurry and also give lagoons their bubble gum-pink coloration. North Carolina has 9.7 million pigs that produce 10 billion gallons of manure annually. [25]

Obesity and fast-food are part of the dysfunction of "*ra*." The Holy One corrected Jonah after the people of Nineveh repented and mentioned the importance of the animals that fasted:

---

[25] https://www.nytimes.com/2018/09/19/climate/florence-hog-farms.html

> And should not I pity Nineveh, that great city, in which there are more than 120,000 persons who do not know their right hand from their left, and also much cattle?
>
> –Jonah 4:11, ESV

Through ignorance, some scream and yell at Satan to get off their bodies while continuing to consume foods that are processed and go against all the commandments in the Bible for agriculture. Healing comes through repentance and obedience. Part of the Holy One's instructions for a blessed life involves the earth resting in the seventh year. We must invest in cleaning and caring for the planet and our physical and mental health.

One cause for mental illness listed in the Bible is pride and idolatry. In the Book of Daniel, King Nebuchadnezzar had a dream that disturbed him, and he sought the magicians and the soothsayers to interpret it, but they were not able. Daniel, otherwise known as *Belteshazzar*, interprets it for him. Every race, language, tribe, kingdom, and nation that formed this king's enormous and diverse empire had sworn adherence to Nebuchadnezzar. He was powerful, but suddenly, Nebuchadnezzar had troubling dreams and visions. The king had dreamt of a tree that grew and was strong and whose height reached up to heaven.

Tom Bradford, Pastor, and Torah Scholar from *The Seed of Abraham Fellowship,* compares the tree in the Garden of Eden to Nebuchadnezzar's dream in his teaching *Daniel, Lesson 4*:

> The Tree of life was at the center of the Garden of Eden, which itself was at the center of the earth. The tree provided good food for the world's first inhabitants, it was beautiful, and it was associated with the Tigris and Euphrates Rivers. Notice how Nebuchadnezzar's dream tree was at the center of the earth, provided food for the world's inhabitants, was beautiful and it was located in Babylon on the Euphrates River not far from the Tigris.
>
> CJB, Revelation 22:1, Next the angel showed me the river of the water of life, sparkling like crystal, flowing from the throne of God and of the Lamb. Between the main street and the river was the Tree of Life producing twelve kinds of fruit, a different kind every month; and the leaves of the tree were for healing the nations-
>
> The future Tree of Life will be at the location of the earthly throne of God's Kingdom; Nebuchadnezzar's dream-tree is at the location of the earthly throne of the King of the heathen world. The leaves of the Tree of life were for healing the nations, meaning gentile nations. The leaves of the dream-tree were for the benefit of the world's gentile nations. [26]

---

[26] https://www.torahclass.com/old-testament-studies-tc/1816-old-testament-studies-daniel/1437-lesson-12-daniel-4-cont

Later in the dream, the king heard a voice from heaven cry out to cut down the tree and to leave its stump:

> But leave the stump of its roots in the earth, bound with a band of iron and bronze, amid the tender grass of the field. Let him be wet with the dew of heaven. Let his portion be with the beasts in the grass of the earth. Let his mind be changed from a man's and let a beast's mind be given to him; and let seven periods of time pass over him.
>
> –Daniel 4:15-16, ESV

Interestingly, chapter 4 of Daniel is narrated by the pagan king, Nebuchadnezzar. We learn that Satan did not give Nebuchadnezzar insanity or a beastly nature. Nor was Satan capable of giving this king dreams and visions. The Father allowed the tree or kingdom to be cut down due to Nebuchadnezzar's pride. Nebuchadnezzar had dominion over the entire earth.

Daniel interprets the dream and tells Nebuchadnezzar that the tree represents him and his kingdom. The dream did not come to fruition until a year later when the king began to boast with great arrogance. Metaphorically, we see the kingdoms of the world being cut off by the coming of the great King, *Yeshua Ha Mashiach*, our Messiah:

> And the king answered and said, "Is not this great Babylon, which I have built by my mighty power as a royal

residence and for the glory of my majesty?" While the words were still in the king's mouth, there fell a voice from heaven, "O King Nebuchadnezzar, to you it is spoken: The kingdom has departed from you, and you shall be driven from among men, and your dwelling shall be with the beasts of the field. And you shall be made to eat grass like an ox, and seven periods of time shall pass over you, until you know that the Most High rules the kingdom of men and gives it to whom he will." Immediately the word was fulfilled against Nebuchadnezzar. He was driven from among men and ate grass like an ox, and his body was wet with the dew of heaven till his hair grew as long as eagles' feathers, and his nails were like birds' claws.

–Daniel 4:30-33, ESV

Adonai allowed Nebuchadnezzar to go insane for seven years until his understanding returned. Seven is the number of completion. This represents the Feast of Trumpets when the Messiah is said to return to set up His Kingdom--an everlasting kingdom. At that time, all the kings of the earth will bow before the true King of Kings.

This great king Nebuchadnezzar lived among the beasts eating grass like an animal. The Holy One turned him over to his flesh nature until it was full-blown, and he repented. If Adonai puts insanity on a person, how can it be cast out? This goes back to the Apostle Paul's remedy for those who have backslidden:

> It is actually reported that there is sexual immorality among you, and of a kind that is intolerable even among pagans: A man has his father's wife. And you are proud! Shouldn't you rather have been stricken with grief and have removed from your fellowship the man who did this? Although I am absent from you in body, I am present with you in spirit, and I have already pronounced judgment on the one who did this, just as if I were present. When you are assembled in the name of our Lord Jesus and I am with you in spirit, along with the power of the Lord Jesus, hand this man over to Satan for the destruction of the flesh, so that his spirit may be saved on the Day of the Lord.
>
> –I Corinthians 5:1-5, BSB

We are told by Yeshua in the gospel of Matthew that the earth will be as the days of Noah and Lot. The kingdoms of the earth and the people will be turned over to their beastly nature.

In modern medicine and psychology, there is an illness termed zoanthropy that deals with a beastly condition:

> Clinical zoanthropy is a rare delusion in which a person believes himself or herself to be an animal (Blom, 2013). In the English translation of his review of the international scientific literature from 1850 onward, Blom (2014) found only 56 cases of clinical zoanthropy.

Approximately 25% of the patients in these cases were diagnosed with schizophrenia, 23% with psychotic depression, and about 20% with bipolar disorder. The patients consisted of 34 men and 22 women, whose symptoms lasted anywhere from a single hour to decades." William F. Doverspike, Ph.D. [27]

The vast number of psychological labels for various conditions is large and overwhelming. Many times, what is needed is deliverance from demonic spirits. Yeshua did not diagnose the condition or prescribe medication, but with power and authority He sent the spirits packing. However, in Nebuchadnezzar s case, the Holy One warned by dream, and allowed the humbling.

Depression is listed as a mental illness by the Department of Psychiatry. Many of Adonai's leading men were suicidal at times. David even feigned mental illness while being hunted by King Saul. Multiple prophets in the Bible were severely depressed and suicidal. Jonah said, "O Lord, please take my life from me for death is better to me than life" (Jonah 4:3, KJV). Elijah cried out, "I've had enough Lord. Take my life; I'm no better than my ancestors!" (I Kings 19:4, NIV). In Numbers 11, Moses says:

> I am not able to carry all this people alone; the burden is too heavy for me. If you will treat me like this, kill me at once, if I find favor in your sight, that I may not see my

---

[27] https://earlychurchhistory.org/politics/nebuchadnezzars-insanity/

wretchedness.

–Numbers 11:14-15, ESV

King David was often weary and depressed:

> I am weary with my moaning; every night I flood my bed with tears; I drench my couch with my weeping.

–Psalm 6:6, ESV

David continues to discuss his grief:

> My heart is in anguish within me; the terrors of death have fallen upon me. Fear and trembling come upon me, and horror overwhelms me.

–Psalm 55:2, 4-5, ESV

The joy of the Lord is our strength, but joy often comes after sorrow through depression and suffering. In II Timothy 1, Paul is suffering in prison. He is getting ready to drink the same cup our Messiah drank and suffer a cruel death. It is believed that Paul was beheaded. Paul mentions living without fear of death but also suffering:

> . . . for God gave us a spirit not of fear but of power and love and self-control. Therefore do not be ashamed of the testimony about our Lord, nor of me his prisoner, but share in suffering for the gospel by the power of God , . . .

–II Timothy 1:7-8, ESV

Suffering wasn't just something the apostles had to endure but also innocent children:

> And a man from the crowd answered Him, "Teacher, I brought You my son, who has a spirit that makes him mute. Whenever it seizes him, it throws him down; he foams at the mouth, grinds his teeth, and becomes stiff. I told Your disciples to drive it out, but they couldn't!"
>
> –Mark 9:17-18, TLV

The man's son in Mark 9 could have epilepsy, a condition often mentioned in the Bible. The word *epilepsy* comes from the ancient Greek *Epilepsia*, from *epilambanein*, meaning "to take hold of, to seize, to attack." [1] Notice the child's father said, "Wherever he takes him, he tears him." There are forty different types of epilepsy. One type, called photosensitive epilepsy, is caused by flashing lights. Scientists believe that it's caused by excessive activity in the brain. Primary reading epilepsy is often triggered when a person reads.

These and many other types of illnesses are complex, but are they demons? Multiple people in the Bible were delivered from demons. Some went on to support Yeshua and walk with him like Mary/Miriam:

> And certain women who had been healed of evil spirits and infirmities—Miriam, the one called Magdalene, out of whom seven demons had gone; Joanna, the wife of Kuza,

Herod's finance minister; Susanna; and many others—were supporting them out of their own resources.

–Luke 8:2-3, TLV

Demoniacs and lunatics or epileptics are listed separately at times:

And his fame went throughout all Syria: and they brought unto him all sick people that were taken with diverse diseases and torments, and those which were possessed with devils, and those which were lunatic, and those that had the palsy; and he healed them.

–Matthew 4:24, KJV

The word lunatic is noteworthy. (Seizures: Strong's Greek 4583: To be a lunatic, be moonstruck, epileptic. Seizures: (σεληνιαζομένους). [28] Lunacy originated from a belief that one could be moon-struck and become mentally deranged. Many superstitions evolved that insinuated that at different phases of the moon, a person could become mad, i.e., werewolves. *The Bible Study Encyclopedia* provides further information:

> The English word "lunatic," which is popular speech signifies a sufferer from any mental derangement, whether periodic or chronic, other than congenital idiocy, appears in the King James Version as a translation of the

---

[28] Strong's Greek: 4583. σεληνιάζομαι (seléniazomai) -- to be moonstruck, spec. be epileptic (supposedly influenced by the moon) (biblehub.com)

Greek word seleniazomai, in the two passages where it occurs. In the Revised Version (British and American), the word has very properly been displaced by the strictly accurate term *epileptic*. [29]

In all references, one can observe and often conclude that those dealing with mental disorders need love and counseling and, yes, at times, deliverance. Mark 5:5 says the demonic man at the tombs cried out and cut himself with stones, and no chains or iron could hold him. But after one touch from the Master Yeshua, he was set free. Several things happened after that:

A) He no longer lived with the dead in a graveyard.

B) He was clothed and in his right mind.

C) He wanted to depart and go with Yeshua.

Perhaps the man had mental issues and his thought pattern was death. Maybe a recording replayed all the wrong he had committed or how he was told he was worthless, stupid, and ugly. He had been living in death and not life. He needed a mental change. He needed garments of light.

Most important to remember is all human beings were created in the image of the Holy One. All life carries the light and divine spark of the Holy One inside their souls. Therefore, we should treat every human being with consideration and respect,

---

[29] https://biblehub.com/topical/l/lunatick.htm

for every human being, whether sick or healthy, is of immense worth. One day we will be changed in the twinkling of an eye. In the meantime, we must ponder mental illnesses in a different light and use compassion for those suffering.

Chapter 12

THE ACCURSED THING

One doctrine prevalent in Christianity is the belief that certain types of material objects can cause a curse to befall a person. The doctrine is taken from the Book of Joshua. "But the children of Israel committed a trespass in the accursed thing" (Joshua 7:1, KJV). The fear stems from objects that could have been used in witchcraft or occult practices. Those working in these types of ministries teach that demonic spirits can manifest when a person purchases or comes in contact with a particular item. Often, under the title of deliverance ministry, pastors are called to come out and bless or perform an exorcism on a certain house of a person with accursed objects. They call it cleaning or ridding the home of demons. This ritual is different from blessing a new home purchased.

One woman I met experienced this clean sweep when a deliverance counselor went through her home, pulling pictures off the walls. Multiple action figures and toys belonging to her son were burned. These ministers teeter on the extreme, going as far as to say that a ceramic owl or a frog in your home can harbor demons. Frogs in Egyptian mythology were worshipped, and they had a frog goddess named Heqet. In Ancient Egypt, the frog was worshipped. They believed it symbolized life and fertility. All frog deities were believed to have had a role in the creation of the earth. Author Dani Rhys of *Symbolsage* Blogsite describes Heqet in her article Heqet--*Egyptian Frog Goddess:*

> Heqet, also known as the 'Frog Goddess' was the Ancient Egyptian goddess of fertility and childbirth. Heqet was usually depicted as a frog, an ancient fertility symbol and was much revered by mortals. Heqet's name was said to have the same roots as the name of the Greek goddess of witchcraft, 'Hecate.' While the actual meaning of her name isn't clear, some believe that it was derived from the Egyptian word 'heqa,' meaning 'scepter,' 'ruler,' and 'magic.' [30]

However, most people who have a ceramic frog in their home are not worshipping it, and besides, the Creator of all gave the frog life.

Some deliverance ministers believe baby dolls are evil and trace them back to Egyptian and Babylonian days. During that era, little girls who had outgrown their dolls would dedicate them to one of the many goddesses. Women were often buried with paddle dolls. Author and teacher Naomi Millburn from the

---

[30] Heqet – Egyptian Frog Goddess - Symbol Sage

college site *Classroom* describes these ancient Egyptian burial practices in her article *What Were Ancient Egyptian Paddle Dolls Used For?*

> People in ancient Egypt were frequently buried with paddle dolls, which were clay or wood statuettes. This burial practice was common during the Eleventh Dynasty, which lasted between the years of 2040 and 1991 B.C. As their name indicates, the dolls had flat bodies shaped similarly to canoe paddles. Archaeologists believe the function of the dolls was to serve as symbols of feminine sexuality and fertility. [31]

A child collecting dolls or carrying a doll around and innocently playing with it is not evil. However, some items identified as dangerous by deliverance ministers, such as Ouija Boards, satanic books, and tarot cards, are symbolic of witchcraft. Those who were converted in Ephesus, burned their books that delved into these dark practices:

> And a number of those who had practiced magic arts brought their books together and burned them in the sight of all. And they counted the value of them and found it came to fifty thousand pieces of silver.
>
> –Acts 19:19, ESV

---

[31] https://classroom.synonym.com/were-ancient-egyptian-paddle-dolls-used-for-9846.html

Other articles could also be considered borderline superstitious by some. For instance, horseshoes, clovers, stars, puppets, and peace symbols seem trivial, but they made a list on several websites connected to deliverance. When a person tries to delve into the spirit world and they have no authority, much harm can come. The occult has always lured people in. Some people are fascinated with conjuring up their long-lost aunt or grandmother they miss, but the Torah/commandments strongly warn against such dabbling. Other people long to know what their future may hold. Instead of seeking the One who created the stars and asking the Holy One to direct them, the person enters a realm of darkness that often brings demonic spirits. And, yes, throughout the Bible, we read of idols and idolatry, but what do we make of Joshua 7 and the objects taken?

Again, one of the scriptures used to incorporate this teaching of "cursed objects" is found in Joshua and speaks of Achan and the accursed thing. In this story, the Holy One spoke to Joshua and told him He was giving him the city of Jericho and that they were to walk around it for seven days. On the seventh day, the priests were instructed to blow the ram's horn, and the walls would come down. Joshua had sent men earlier to spy out the land, and Rahab had hidden them to protect them. Because of her boldness, she and her household were saved when Israel invaded the city of Jericho. Rahab was to hang a scarlet cord in the window and let her family members down to freedom. But Adonai gave them a warning:

> And the city shall be accursed, even it, and all that are therein to the Father; only Rahab the harlot (Inn-keeper) shall live, she and all that are with her in the house, because she hid the messengers that we sent. And you in any wise keep yourselves from the accursed thing, lest ye make yourselves accursed, when ye take of the accursed thing, and make the camp of Israel a curse and trouble it.
>
> –Joshua 6:17-18, KJV

Later, Joshua sent men to spy out the land of Ai. They went in to conquer it but ended up running with their tails between their legs. Adonai told Joshua that Israel had sinned and could not defeat Ai. The reason for their failure to conquer was that they had taken of the accursed thing and even put it amongst their substance. The Father had warned them:

> But you, just keep yourselves from the things under the ban. Otherwise you would make yourselves accursed by taking of the things under the ban, and so you would make the camp of Israel accursed and bring trouble on it. All the silver and gold and vessels of bronze and iron are holy to *Adonai*, and must go into the treasury of *Adonai*.
>
> –Joshua 6:18-19, TLV

In Joshua 7, the men of Israel go up to attack Ai and return, losing 30 some men. The whole camp is filled with fear. Joshua tears his clothing and falls on his face before the Ark of the

Covenant. Joshua and the elders lay prostrate with dust on their heads until evening. Then Joshua asked the Holy One why this had happened? The Father responds and tells Joshua, "Get up! Israel has sinned and disobeyed my covenant that I commanded them." The Lord then makes Joshua aware that someone has taken the accursed things. Joshua rose early and brought the tribe near:

> So Joshua said to Achan, "My son, give glory now to *Adonai*, God of Israel, and give praise to Him, and confess to me now what you have done—hide nothing from me."
>
> Achan responded to Joshua and said: "It's true! I have sinned against *Adonai*, God of Israel! This is what I have done: When I saw among the spoil a beautiful Shinar mantle and 200 shekels of silver and a wedge of gold 50 shekels in weight, I coveted them and took them. Look, they are buried in the ground in the middle of my tent, with the silver under it."
>
> –Joshua 7:19-21, TLV

Achan heard Joshua give the order that all the spoils in Jericho were to be devoted to the Lord. The spoil was to go into the Lord's treasury "All the silver and gold and vessels of bronze and iron are holy to *Adonai*, and must go into the treasury of *Adonai*" (Joshua 6:19, TLV). Jericho was Israel's first victory in Canaan.

The first fruits of the spoils belonged to Adonai. "Bring the best of the firstfruits of your soil to the house of the LORD your God" (Exodus 23:19, ESV). "Honor the LORD with your wealth and with the firstfruits of all your produce;" (Prov. 3:9, ESV). Achan disobeyed and caused everyone to suffer for his covetousness. Clearly, the silver and gold were not cursed because they had belonged to the Amorites; they were cursed because Achan coveted them. They were supposed to be brought into the House of Adonai.

In the New Testament, a married couple meets their death just as Achan along with his whole family. Ananias and his wife Sapphira sold property and kept some of the money back for themselves, then lied to the apostles. The husband is struck dead, and then his wife is questioned and lies:

> "How could you agree to test the Spirit of the Lord?" Peter replied. "Look, the feet of the men who buried your husband are at the door, and they will carry you out also." At that instant she fell down at his feet and died. Then the young men came in and, finding her dead, carried her out and buried her beside her husband. And great fear came over the whole church and all who heard about these events.
>
> –Acts 5:9-11, ESV

Again, as in the previous story, the money was not what brought a curse, it was the lying and deceit. Similarly, when Moses and the children of Israel left Egypt, Adonai told them to plunder the Egyptians. They took their gold and their silver. They melted it down and made the holy articles for the tabernacle:

> The people of Israel had also done as Moses told them, for they had asked the Egyptians for silver and gold jewelry and for clothing. And the LORD had given the people favor in the sight of the Egyptians, so that they let them have what they asked. Thus they plundered the Egyptians.
>
> –Exodus 12:35-36, ESV

Taking the objects for their lust or their own desires like Achan would constitute the sin, not the objects themselves.

In Genesis 31, Jacob is fleeing from his father-in-law, Laban, with his wives, children, and livestock. Jacob had departed unannounced. His wife, Rachel, when leaving, took her father's idols:

> Now Rachel had taken the idols, put them in the camel's saddlebag, and sat on them. So Laban felt around the entire tent but did not find them. She said to her father, "Let not my lord be angry that I cannot rise before you, for I am having the way of women." So he searched but did not find the idols.
>
> –Genesis 31:34-35, TLV

After Jacob departed from Laban and made peace, an angel of Adonai met him, and Jacob said, "This is God's host." Jacob went on to meet his brother Esau whom he had deceived by trickery, gaining his father Isaac's blessing as if he were the firstborn. Yet Jacob had closure and moved on. The Holy One showed up and called Jacob by his new name Israel and blessed him. Nothing horrible happened over these images. We read nowhere of the Lord, nor the angels, warning him to get rid of the idols. They seemed insignificant in the story except to show that Rachel may have wanted to spare her father of his idolatry and planned on disposing of the idols later. The father of faith, Abraham, came from a place of idolatry. Abraham's father was a maker of idols and sold gods of wood and stone:

> Then Joshua said to all the people: "Thus says Adonai, God of Israel: 'From ancient times your fathers—Terah, the father of Abraham and the father of Nahor—lived beyond the River and worshipped other gods.'"
>
> –Joshua 24:2, TLV

Abraham was not under a generational curse or demonic attack over his father's sin but was a man called of Adonai.

A popular website called *Warfare Pray* lists objects that they claim can bring sickness, disease, and demon infiltration. Some of the items listed are owls, unicorns, frogs, horseshoes, and articles from other countries such as Africa, China, Japan, and

America, including Indian artifacts. The website warns against the popular goose with the blue ribbon around its neck found on many a kitchen canister. They claim this duck is an Egyptian god. They believe dolls originate from voodoo. Among other beliefs is that a birthstone ring symbolizes astrology and can invite demons. This site causes fear in the Body of Messiah. They encourage the reader to pray specific prayers throughout the day. These prayers must be prayed before entering the office, grocery store, anyone else's home, and even after talking on the phone, etc. A partial prayer listed after contact with any person says, *"In Jesus' name, I command every demon that has followed me, was sent to me, or transferred to me, to leave now."* Warfare Prayer website warns people not to open their web pages or check their mail without a prayer of protection. What a fearful way to live! They have prayers they pray before they go to sleep. If a sharp pain arises, they believe a demon or voodoo pin is being stabbed into them. Prayers are said to break curses and demons off their food before eating. To have an outsider come in for home repair means serious house cleaning and renouncement prayers after they leave. Below is a prayer they repeat after coming in contact with someone:

> *As your war club and weapons of war, I break down, undam, and blow up all walls of protection around all witches, warlocks, wizards, Satanists, sorcerers, and I break the power of all curses, hexes, vexes, spells, charms, fetishes, psychic prayers, psychic thoughts, all*

> *witchcraft, sorcery, magic, voodoo, all mind control, jinxes, potions, bewitchments, death, destruction, sickness, pain, torment, psychic power, psychic warfare, prayer chains, incense and candle burning, incantations, chanting, ungodly blessings, voodoo, crystals, root works, and everything else being sent my way, or my family member's way, or any deliverance ministries' way, and I return it, and the demons to the sender, one hundredfold, and I bind it to them by the blood of Jesus.*[32]

These types of prayers and doctrines are toxic. These words inject fear instead of the power of Yeshua, our Messiah. He who the Son sets free is free. Believers in Messiah do not have to walk around in fear and pray continuously against a demon or demonic infestation. Our focus should be on the Holy One and on loving our neighbor as ourselves. Our eyes should be focused on the light, not the darkness. Anything focused on grows. Reading our Father's Word washes us, and we are convicted of ridding the unclean things from our lives. It's often not the objects in our homes but the objects in our hearts that need more attention.

---

[32] https://warfarepray.weebly.com/prayers-against-occult.html

Chapter 13

THE SINS OF THE FATHERS

When I became terribly sick with what one neurologist said was multiple sclerosis, I had many questions as to why. Several possible reasons flooded my mind. One was a doctrine I had been taught in church concerning "generational curses." I was upset about this and wondered how to break such a curse. I prayed with tears in my eyes and asked the Holy One for mercy, but my sickness only continued to worsen.

I became relentlessly tormented with muscle spasms and slurring of speech. One morning, as I tried to get out of bed, my legs buckled under me. The pain and suffering were almost unbearable. I again began to wonder what curse had been brought upon me. As I continued to decline, I cried out for days, finally asking, "Adonai, am I going to die?" I will never forget crying and the fear I felt. I opened my Bible that day after asking the Father if my time was up. The first scripture my eyes landed on said, "This sickness is not unto death but for the glory of God" (John 11:4, KJV). As I write these words, I know that if it were not for this sickness, I would have never had the ability to study His Word so intently. We must remember that all things work together for good. Joseph's betrayal, rejection, pit, and prison time equipped and humbled him, preparing him for second in command of all Egypt. Suffering is the key that unlocks humility and the anointing.

Suffering is not an attack from Satan. Not even in the Book of Job. "Then the LORD said to Satan, "Have you considered My servant Job? For there is no one on earth like him, a man who is blameless and upright, who fears God and shuns evil" (Job 1:8, BSB). Permission is given by Adonai for the "adversary" to allow suffering as long as he spares Job's life. "Very well," said the LORD to Satan. "Everything he has is in your hands, but you must not lay a hand on the man himself" (Job 1:12, BSB). Over and over again, we are told that suffering brings maturity. Yeshua suffered:

> Although he was a son, he learned obedience through what he suffered.
>
> –Hebrews 5:8, ESV

Suffering is a sign that we are His children:

> For the Lord disciplines the one He loves, and He chastises every son He receives.
>
> –Hebrews 12:6, BSB

Once we give our life to Yeshua, we are crucified with Him. We are a new creation and heirs:

> "For ye have not received the spirit of bondage again to fear; but ye have received the spirit of adoption, whereby we cry Abba, Father." He goes on to say, "The spirit itself beareth witness with our spirit that we are the children of God. And if children, then heirs."
>
> —Romans 8:15-17, KJV

Many denominations today pray for generational curses to be broken off individuals. Some believe that these curses can cause numerous afflictions of sickness and disease. They claim generational curses cause poverty, mental and emotional breakdowns, miscarriages, and the list continues. Many interpret Deuteronomy 5:8-10 and Exodus 20:4-6 to teach "generational curses." These curses they believe fall on the children resulting from their fathers' sins. There are entire ministries devoted to helping people break free from these generational curses over their lives. This doctrine originates from some scriptures found in the Old Testament (*Tanakh*) concerning idolatry:

> Do not make for yourself a graven image—no image of what is in the heavens above or on the earth beneath or in the water under the earth. Do not bow down to them or worship them. For I, *Adonai* your God, am a jealous God,

> visiting the iniquity of the fathers on the children and on the third and fourth generation of those who hate Me, but showing lovingkindness to a thousand generations of those who love Me and keep My *mitzvot*.
>
> −Deuteronomy 5:8-10, TLV

The word mitzvot pertains to the commandments of the Holy One. There is another passage quite like this one found in Exodus that is often used to promote generational curses passed down from the fathers:

> You shall not make for yourself a carved image, or any likeness of anything that is in heaven above, or that is in the earth beneath, or that is in the water under the earth. You shall not bow down to them or serve them, for I the LORD your God am a jealous God, visiting the iniquity of the fathers on the children to the third and the fourth generation of those who hate me, but showing steadfast love to thousands of those who love me and keep my commandments.
>
> −Exodus 20:4-6, ESV

The visiting "the iniquity of the fathers" concerned those who hated Adonai. Notice the so called generational curse in Exodus 20 was placed by the Holy One. Many in leadership pray and renounce generational curses over individuals, but if the Holy One placed them, and He said He would place the curse upon the third and fourth generation according to Exodus 20:4-6, how can they be broken? The following is a hypothetical story:

> A person had a great, great grandfather who was a Freemason and involved in sorcery. This person learns his grandfather was into sorcery. However, this person was utterly oblivious to any of this. The said person became born anew and recently baptized. Weeks later, the person with this newfound faith in Yeshua grows tired, and his eyesight becomes blurry. The person visits an ophthalmologist, and the ophthalmologist diagnoses a rare eye disease that will soon cause complete blindness. The person goes to the deliverance minister or pastor, who starts questioning him about family history. The person then inquires, asking his parents if there was any witchcraft in the family—the family concerned responds by explaining that Grandpa Carter dabbled in the occult. The person goes back to the minister, who then has the person renounce Satan, adding a long list of generational curses. The minister has him repeat repetitious prayers. The new believer suddenly feels horrible that the Lord has placed a curse of blindness because of his ancestor's sins. He feels spiritually lost and sick inside. The person was so joyous just weeks before but is now completely floored. Sadly, he will soon be completely blind and believe it is the result of all his ancestors' sins.

The above story is hypothetical, but it is becoming more realistic in some assemblies today. What did our Master Yeshua say when He was tested about generational curses?

> And Jesus passed by and saw a man which was blind from birth. And his disciples asked him, saying, Master, who did sin, this man, or his parents, that he was born blind? Jesus answered, neither hath this man sinned, nor his parents: but that the works of God should be made manifest in him.
>
> –John 9:1-3, KJV

The disciples had been indoctrinated with Hellenism. Greek thought affected the first-century world of Yeshua and His disciples. Hellenistic ideas were part of the culture and had been creeping in for some time. In Greek thought, an innocent child could not be born blind without sin from the parents.

Moses had an inability to speak well and brought his weakness to Adonai. Adonai said: "Who hath made man's mouth? Or who maketh the dumb or deaf, or the seeing, or the blind? Have not I the Father?" (Exodus 4:11, KJV). In John 9, the Lord used blindness to showcase His power and glory. The Holy One blinded Paul for three days on the road to Damascus before setting him apart for service:

> In a vision he (Paul) has seen a man named Ananias come and place his hands on him to restore his sight. "Lord,"

Ananias answered, "I have heard many reports about this man and all the harm he has done to your holy people in Jerusalem. And he has come here with authority from the chief priests to arrest all who call on your name." But the Lord said to Ananias, "Go! This man is my chosen instrument to proclaim my name to the Gentiles and their kings and to the people of Israel. I will show him how much he must suffer for my name."

–Acts 9:12-16, NIV

If a person becomes blind or sick with a disease, the Bible is noticeably clear on what to do:

Is any sick among you? Let him call for the elders of the church; and let them pray over him, anointing him with oil in the name of the Lord: And the prayer of faith shall save the sick, and the Lord shall raise him up; and if he has committed sins, they shall be forgiven him.

–James 5:14-15, KJV

James 5 says, "If he committed sins," not if he or his father or grandfather had committed sins. James 5 gives no instructions to break generational curses off of the sick person. Generational traits, personalities, hereditary diseases, or even spiritual issues are not to be ignored, but many things affect each individual situation. Sickness and disease have become more prevalent as the world continues to become overpopulated. Man has not kept the instructions placed in the Torah for a healthy, vital life. Childhood diseases, like measles or whooping cough, need a sizeable population to emerge and be transmitted. The Covid virus works the same. Droplets spread to others and many times to righteous people who are by no means under a curse. Many of the modern diseases stem from poor sanitation in crowded cities, fast food, and obesity. A person may develop diabetes, become diagnosed with cancer or heart disease, but that is not because he or she is under a curse. It may be because people do not eat right or take care of their body, or it may be hereditary.

Eli, the high priest, was righteous, but his sons were bent on evil. They were not wicked because of a generational curse, but scriptures suggest that Eli did not discipline them: "Eli's sons were scoundrels; they had no regard for the Lord" (I Samuel 2:12, TLV). The Lord spoke to Eli concerning his honor towards his sons over Adonai:

> Why do you kick at My sacrifice and My offering which I have commanded in My dwelling, and honor your sons above Me, by fattening yourselves with the choicest of every offering of Israel My people?
>
> −I Samuel 2:29, TLV

Eli taught Samuel the prophet from a tender age. Samuel became a prophet and judge over Israel walking in all the ways of the Holy One, but Samuel's sons were not righteous. His sons were similar to Eli's, the man who raised him up in Adonai's house:

> When Samuel became old, he made his sons judges over Israel. The name of his firstborn son was Joel, and the name of his second, Abijah; they were judges in Beersheba. Yet his sons did not walk in his ways but turned aside after gain. They took bribes and perverted justice.
>
> –I Samuel 8:1-3, ESV

One doctrine prevalent in the charismatic churches proclaims generational curses cause poverty, bondage, and sickness. The curses listed in Deuteronomy and Exodus were brought upon the people who hated the Lord and did not keep His commandments. The false doctrine of generational curses makes the blood of Yeshua weak. This type of teaching stifles people, and places blame on a curse instead of correction, following the commandments for a blessed life.

Disobedience concerning the commandments causes multiple issues, but a person the Messiah has set free is free, regardless of their parent's sins. Why would a loving Father who sent His Son impart suffering to a believer over the generations that hated Him? Would God send His Son to die for us, but with stipulations that it does not cover Grandpa Carter's sins of sorcery? Are we to pay for our ancestors' wickedness? The Holy One answers the question by responding to Ezekiel:

> Yet you say, "Why should not the son suffer for the iniquity of the father?" When the son has done what is just and right, and has been careful to observe all my statutes, he shall surely live. The soul who sins shall die. The son shall not suffer for the iniquity of the father, nor the father suffer for the iniquity of the son. The righteousness of the righteous shall be upon himself, and the wickedness of the wicked shall be upon himself.
>
> –Ezekiel 18:18-20, ESV

Most people need counseling and love, not fear that they are under a generational curse that needs to be broken. The Father sent His Word to heal us, and if we get enough of His Word in us, we will not want to sin against Him.

For many, a favorite book in the Bible is the Book of Ruth. If any book can throw the generational curse theory out of the water, it is this book. Ruth was a Moabitess. The Moabites descended from a son born of Lot, conceived through drunkenness with his daughters (incest). The Moabite people worshiped mainly the god "Chemosh," to whom they sacrificed their children. Dr. Judd H. Burton, historian and anthropologist, describes the origin of this worship:

> Chemosh was the national deity of the Moabites whose name most likely meant "destroyer," "subduer," or "fish god." While he is most readily associated with the

Moabites, according to Judges 11:24, he seems to have been the national deity of the Ammonites as well. His presence in the Old Testament world was well known, as his cult was imported to Jerusalem by King Solomon (1 Kings 11:7). The Hebrew scorn for his worship was evident in a curse from the scriptures: "the abomination of Moab." King Josiah destroyed the Israelite branch of the cult (2 Kings 23). [33]

Ruth's mother-in-law, Naomi, lost her husband and two sons. Naomi was left heartbroken and grief-stricken. She only had her two daughter-in-law's, Ruth and Orpah. Naomi was making her way from Moab back to her homeland, Bethlehem. Orpah kissed her mother-in-law, but Ruth cleaved unto her and declared that the God of Naomi, the God of Abraham, Isaac, and Jacob would be her God. Ruth is in the genealogy of the Messiah. Not only is Ruth in His genealogy, but other women are mentioned: Rahab, Bathsheba, who committed adultery with King David, and Tamar, who dressed up as a prostitute and slept with her father-in-law Judah. If Ruth's father and her grandfather were Moabites and worshipped Chemos, sacrificing to other gods, she should have been under this generational curse, but she was not.

Those in deliverance often try to blame every sin and problem of the flesh on a curse passed down. But this is just not

---

[33] https://www.thoughtco.com/chemosh-lord-of-the-moabites-117630

biblical. If a person goes out and gets drunk and has a wreck, killing someone, the person reaps the consequences. If a person commits fornication or adultery and contracts an STD, isn't that a result of the seeds they planted? Miriam gossiped and was removed from the camp. After seven days, she was brought back into the community. This is a picture of a loving Father who is merciful and just and offers forgiveness. The Holy One judges each of us according to our ways:

> Therefore I will judge you, O house of Israel, every one according to his ways, declares the Lord GOD. Repent and turn from all your transgressions, lest iniquity be your ruin. Cast away from you all the transgressions that you have committed, and make yourselves a new heart and a new spirit! Why will you die, O house of Israel? For I have no pleasure in the death of anyone, declares the Lord GOD; so turn, and live.
>
> –Ezekiel 18:30-32, ESV

Many times, what Christians believe to be a curse is actually a test. Paul informs us that we are heirs and made new in Messiah:

> Therefore if anyone is in Messiah, he is a new creation. The old things have passed away; behold, all things have become new.
>
> –II Corinthians 5:17, TLV

When we are born again, we are new creations. It does not matter what our fathers did. Ruth became an Israelite and married Boaz. Negative behavior patterns such as alcoholism, addictions of all types, abuse, and anger tend to repeat themselves. However, this is not due to a curse passed down, but learned behaviors. Children often mimic what they hear and see, but that is not always the case. Remember, Eli and Samuel were righteous, but their sons were not. However, many things are passed down due to traumatized parents, like the children of those who survived the holocaust. Author John Rogers of *The Sun* covers epigenetic inheritance:

> Ivan Rektor, a neurologist at the university said the results indicated there was a deterioration in the brains of the children of camp survivors. The research would appear to support the idea of "epigenetic inheritance" which suggests environmental factors can impact the genes of your children. Professor Rektor said: "After more than 70 years, the impact of surviving the Holocaust on brain function is significant. "We revealed substantial differences in the brain structures involved in the processing of emotion, memory and social cognition, in higher level of stress but also of post-traumatic growth between Holocaust survivors and controls. [34]

---

[34] Holocaust survivors' kids and grandchildren have inherited concentration camp 'brain damage' that will affect their learning for generations, study finds | The Sun

Environmental exposures and personal interactions control epigenetic changes. When the exposures change, there is a possibility that the epigenetic changes might be reversed. Men and women who have been through PTSD and trauma can bring healing to their brains through the Light of Yeshua and the power of His Word. If anyone is in Messiah Yeshua, that person is a new creation. Like the man at the tombs in Luke 8, he was cutting himself and crying out in torment, but with one touch of our Master Yeshua's Hand, the man was clothed and in his right mind. Behold, the new man had come! The old man with all his trauma had passed away.

Spirits Unveiled: Book Two

Closing

Spirits Unveiled highlights the sovereign Creator of all the heavens and the earth. The earth cries out. Everything happening on the earth sends forth a vibration and makes a sound. In Genesis 18, the Holy One hears the sounds, and He sees:

> Then *Adonai* said, "The outcry against Sodom and Gomorrah is great indeed, and their sin is very grievous indeed. I want to go down now, and see if they deserve destruction, as its outcry has come to Me. And if not, I will know."
>
> —Genesis 18:20-21, TLV

It is after this chapter that the Lord sends angelic hosts to Lot:

> Now the two angels arrived at Sodom in the evening, and Lot was sitting in the gateway of the city. When Lot saw them, he got up to meet them, bowed facedown.
>
> —Genesis 19:1, BSB

These wondrous angels we read about are agents with assignments. We learn that angels war, send forth pestilence, stand with swords, and surround armies on horses. Not only are angels sent forth from Yahweh, but at times other spirits are. "Now the Spirit of the LORD left Saul, and an evil spirit from the LORD terrified him" (I Samuel 16:14, NASB). Time and again, the Holy One is in control or has allowed men like Job to go through suffering. All suffering has a purpose. The apostle Paul would certainly agree. In Acts 9, Saul is still breathing out threats and having the believers in Messiah arrested. On the road traveling, Yeshua speaks to Saul, corrects him, and when Saul gets up, he is blind and cannot see. But who caused this malady? Again, the One in control, the Lord of Hosts:

> "Saul, why are you persecuting Me?" And he said, "Who are You, Lord?" And He said, "I am Jesus whom you are persecuting, but get up and enter the city, and it will be told to you what you must do." The men who traveled with him stood speechless, hearing the voice but seeing no one. Saul got up from the ground, and though his eyes were open, he could see nothing; and leading him by the hand, they brought him into Damascus. And for three days he was without sight, and neither ate nor drank.
>
> –Acts 9:4-9, NASB

Both men named Saul (*Sha'ul*), suffered. Both men were struck in some fashion, yet the Father is merciful, abounding in love, not wanting anyone to suffer. Time and again, He sends angels to help His chosen and also little maidservants. Hagar, Abraham's concubine and mother of his son Ishmael, is met by the Angel of the Lord at a well. Hagar wanders the desert until she has no means to feed her son or herself. Exhausted, Hagar abandons her son so she won't have to watch him die and sits away from the boy to cry. However, her cries are not what reach the heavens, it is her son's cries. This is the second time the Angel of Yahweh speaks to Hagar. He opens her eyes, and she sees the well of Beersheba:

> And God heard the voice of the boy, and the angel of God called to Hagar from heaven and said to her, "What troubles you, Hagar? Fear not, for God has heard the voice of the boy where he is."
>
> –Genesis 21:17, ESV

Strangely, many times, the angel of the Lord appears to be Yeshua Himself. In Daniel, three Hebrew men are thrown into a fiery furnace that has been heated seven times hotter because they would not bow nor worship other gods or graven images:

> Then Nebuchadnezzar, the king was astounded and stood up quickly; he said to his counselors, "Was it not three men that we threw bound into the middle of the fire?" They replied to the king, "Absolutely, O king." He responded, "Look! I see four men untied and walking

about in the middle of the fire unharmed, and the appearance of the fourth is like a son of the gods!"

–Daniel 3:24-25, NASB

The above passage from Daniel 3 clearly shows that angels are given assignments to protect the righteous. Angels in Acts 5 open prison doors:

> They laid hands on the apostles and put them in a public prison. But during the night, an angel of the Lord opened the gates of the prison, and leading them out, he said, "Go, stand and speak to the people in the temple area the whole message of this Life." Upon hearing this, they entered into the temple area about daybreak and began to teach.

–Acts 5:18-21, NASB

We are told to be careful, as we may be entertaining angels unawares. "Do not be forgetful of hospitality, for through this, some have entertained angels unawares" (Hebrews 13:2, BSB). Be sure to take a second glance at a stranger needing help because these Holy visitors may show up disguised as humans. Angels gain new prominence in Ezekiel with cherubim and chariots. The Book of Daniel places names to angels, wherein the Biblical account of Samson, when his father asked the angel for its name, receives a rebuke:

> And the angel of the LORD said unto him, Why askest thou thus after my name, seeing it is secret?
>
> –Judges 13:18 KJB

By the time of the early Hellenistic period, angels and intermediary spirits had exploded. Before the Dead Sea scrolls, Daniel was the first to enlighten us with more information concerning these spirit beings.

I hope you are enjoying this Four-Part Series, *Unmasking the Unseen*. In Book One, *Satan Unmasked*, we looked at Satan with a more Hebraic lens, the history of Satan, and how he has evolved. This book, Book Two, *Spirits Unveiled*, delved into all things concerning angelic beings, demonic spirits, witchcraft, sorcery, and deliverance. In Book Three, *Wolves Unseen*, we will examine wolves in sheep's clothing, cults, the tithe, and the feasts of Adonai. The Series ends with Book Four, *King Revealed*.

Blessings,

Tekoa Manning

DON'T GO YET!

Thank you for reading Book Two, *Spirits Unveiled*, of the *Unmasking the Unseen Series*. I hope you already enjoyed Book One, *Satan Unmasked*, and continue with Book Three, *Wolves Unseen*, and Book Four, *King Revealed*. These books have been a labor of love and have taken years of research to complete. Your feedback and thoughts are important to me.

COULD YOU HELP ME?

Please leave me an honest review.
It would mean so much to me and help with our ministry to orphans in India and Malawi.

Please also refer this Book Series, *Unmasking the Unseen*, to those who may benefit from it. For updates and new book releases, go to Tekoamanning.com.

Blessings & Shalom,
Tekoa Manning
Manning the Gate Publishing LLC

SOURCES

1. Sauter, Megan, (2022) Lilith in the Bible and Mythology. Retrieved 9-25-2022. Lilith in the Bible and Mythology - Biblical Archaeology Society

2. Jewish Virtual Library Encyclopaedia Judaica. (2008)The Gale Group. Dibbuk (Dybbuk) Retrieved on 7-12-2017. Dibbuk (Dybbuk) (jewishvirtuallibrary.org)

3. Hannah, History Things. Take A Look Into the Dark History of Ventriloquism. (12-20-2020). Retrieved 2-12-2022. Take A Look Into the Dark History of Ventriloquism (historythings.com)

4. Bible Hub. (2004-2022) Kidneys. Retrieved 8-12-2021. Topical Bible: Kidneys (biblehub.com)

5. Jourdan, Lenoir Nicole. (10-28-2020) How witchcraft became a multi-billion dollar industry. Retrieved on 9-8-2021. How witchcraft became a multi-billion dollar industry (theconversation.com)

6. Schaeffer, Francis, Az Quotes. (1982). The Complete Works of Francis A. Schaeffer: A Christian view of the west. Retrieved 9-7-2022. Francis Schaeffer quote: If there is no absolute moral standard, then one cannot... (azquotes.com)

7. Ludwig Blau, Kaufmann Kohler. (2002-2021). ANGELOLOGY, Jewish Encyclopedia. Retrieved 3-12-2020. ANGELOLOGY - JewishEncyclopedia.com

8.   Olyan M. Saul, Siebeck Mohr (Paul). (10-15-2009). A Thousand Thousands Served Him: Exegesis and the Naming of Angels in Ancient Judaism. Retrieved on 9-12-2022. Saul M. Olyan. A Thousand Thousands Served Him: Exegesis and the Naming of Angels in Ancient Judaism. Texte und Studien zum Antiken Judentum 36. Tübingen: J. C. B. Mohr (Paul Siebeck), 1993. xiv, 148 pp. | AJS Review | Cambridge Core

9.   Scott, Brad. The Wildbranch Ministry. (no date) The Tabernacle, The Ark, Part II. Retrieved on 8-14-2022. The Tabernacle-4 — The WildBranch Ministry

10.   Swanbrow, Diane Ph.D. (11- 16-2011). The history of angels: U-M research. Retrieved on 6-12-2022. The history of angels: U-M research (phys.org)

11.   Abarim Publications — first published on 2011-05-31; last updated on 2022-05-13. Seraphim meaning in Biblical Hebrew. Retrieved on 7-07-2022. Seraphim | The amazing word Seraphim: meaning and etymology (abarim-publications.com)

12.   The Book of Enoch PDF. Chapter 48. (2022). Retrieved on 9-27-2022. Chapter 48 [1] – The Book of Enoch (book-ofenoch.com)

13.   Beezlebub - Hebrew Bible. (2022). Retrieved on 8-23-2022. Beezlebub - Hebrew Bible (liquisearch.com)

14.   Abarim Publications — first published on 2014-05-05; last updated on 2022-05-13. The Name Legion: Summary. Retrieved on 9-28-2022. Legion | The amazing name Legion: meaning and etymology (abarim-publications.com)

15. Peck, Scott. (6/14/2019). "People of the Lie" The Hope for Healing Human Evil. Retrieved on 9-28-2022. "People of the Lie" by M. Scott Peck — smatterings.net

16. Yaron Yadan (09/27/2006). Magic in the Talmud. Retrieved on 9-29-2022. Magic in the Talmud | Daat Emet

17. Rabbi Enkin, Ari. United With Israel. (2-18-2015). Judaism & Demons: Does the Torah Address the Occult? Retrieved on 9-28-2022. Judaism and Demons: Does the Torah Address the Occult? | United with Israel

18. Bentorah, Chaim and Laura. (Jun 9, 2014). Biblical Hebrew, WORD STUDY – HEALING HANDKERCHIEFS. Retrieved on 10-01-2022. WORD STUDY – HEALING HANDKERCHIEFS | Chaim Bentorah

19. First Fruits of Zion. (no date). The Power to Bind and Loose. Retrieved on 11-01-2022. The Power to Bind and Loose | Gospel Insights | Torah Portions (ffoz.org)

20. Kaufmann, Kohler. Jewish Encyclopedia (no date). BINDING AND LOOSING (Hebrew, "asar we-hittir"; Aramean, "asar we-shera"): Retrieved on 11-10-2022. BINDING AND LOOSING - JewishEncyclopedia.com

21. Nauert, Rick PhD. Psych Central. Bitterness Can Make You Sick? (8-11-2011). Retrieved on 10-09-2022. Emotional Health and Personal Growth Resources (psychcentral.com)

22. Moen, Skip Ph.D. (January 5, 2013) Hebrew Word Study. Rooftop Faith. Retrieved on 10-01-2022. Rooftop Faith – Hebrew Word Study | Skip Moen

23. National Center for Chronic Disease Prevention and Health Promotion, Division of Population Health. (June 28, 2021). What is mental health? Retrieved on 11-12-2022. About Mental Health (cdc.gov)

24. Benner, Jeff A. (1999-2022) Ancient Hebrew Research Center. Good. Retrieved on 3-16-2020. Hebrew Word Definition: Good | AHRC (ancient-hebrew.org)

25. Pierre-Louis, Kendra (09-19- 2018 Lagoons of Pig Waste Are Overflowing After Florence. Yes, That's as Nasty as It Sounds. Retrieved on 10-4-2022. Lagoons of Pig Waste Are Overflowing After Florence. Yes, That's as Nasty as It Sounds. - The New York Times (nytimes.com)

26. Bradford Tom, The Seed of Abraham Ministry. Torah Class-Daniel 12. (11-28-2020). Retrieved on 6-19-2019. Lesson 1 Intro - Torah Class

27. Silver, Sweeny, Sandra. Early Church History (no date). NEBUCHADNEZZAR'S INSANITY—WHAT WAS IT? (9-2-2021. Retrieved on 10-02-2022. Nebuchadnezzar's Insanity—What Was It? (earlychurchhistory.org)

28. Bible Hub. Strong's Concordance. (2004-2022). 4583. Seléniazomai—seizure. Retrieved Retrieved on 1-14-2020. Strong's Greek: 4583. σεληνιάζομαι (seléniazomai) -- to be moonstruck, spec. be epileptic (supposedly influenced by the moon) (biblehub.com)

29. Bible Hub. Bible Encyclopdia. (2004-2022). Lunatick. Retrieved on 4-2-2022. Topical Bible: Lunatick (biblehub.com)

30. Rhys, Dani, Symbol sage logo. (2022) Heqet – Egyptian Frog Goddess. Retrieved on 6-12-2020.

31. Millburn, Naomi. Leaf Group. (No date). What Were Ancient Egyptian Paddle Dolls Used. Retrieved on 10-25-2022. The Ancient Greek View of the Male Body (synonym.com)

32. Faith Outreach, Warfare Prayers. (no date) Retrieved on 12-6-2021. Prayers against Occult - WARFARE PRAYERS (weebly.com)

33. Burton H. Judd, Learn Religions. (08- 07- 2019). Chemosh: Ancient God of Moabites. Retrieved on 8-12-2020. Chemosh: Ancient God of Moabites (learnreligions.com)

34. Rogers, Jon. (7-01-2019). News Group Newspaper. SCARRED DNA--Holocaust survivors' kids and grandchildren have inherited concentration camp 'brain damage' that will affect their learning for generations, study finds. Retrieved on 11-10-2022. Holocaust survivors' kids and grandchildren have inherited concentration camp 'brain damage' that will affect their learning for generations, study finds | The Sun

www.ingramcontent.com/pod-product-compliance
Lightning Source LLC
Chambersburg PA
CBHW070121110526
44587CB00017BA/2904